New Trends in
the Teaching of English in
Secondary Schools

NEW TRENDS IN CURRICULUM AND INSTRUCTION SERIES

New Trends in the Teaching of English in Secondary Schools

WILLIAM H. EVANS
Southern Illinois University
Carbondale Campus

JERRY L. WALKER
University of Illinois
Champaign-Urbana Campus

RAND MCNALLY & COMPANY • CHICAGO

Preface

A little book on new trends in the teaching of English in secondary schools invites immediate attention. Discoveries in linguistics and grammar alone would easily fill a dozen books the size of this one.

There is no attempt at completeness in these pages. College specialists in English education, English supervisors, and English teachers who have watched new developments closely and have experimented in an effort to discover those which will be of greatest benefit to students in the secondary schools should have much to add to this book.

But it seems timely to glance back for achievements of significance, to consider where English is today, and to set down an outline of new trends. Because new developments now crowd the minds of all persons who are concerned about the teaching of English in the secondary schools, there is need for such an overview.

If this book has any special readers, they are experienced English teachers who have been working very hard at teaching English from day to day and have only sampled from the overwhelming array of innovations and new knowledge; students who are considering the teaching of English as a profession; beginning English teachers who stand between their college preparation and classroom experience; and anxious parents and school administrators who have been caught up in the new mathematics, the new science, the new study of foreign languages, and are now being asked to look more closely at what is called the "new English" in their schools.

W.H.E.
J.L.W.

Contents

New Trends in
the Teaching of English in
Secondary Schools

I

English as a Subject:
A Case History

New developments in the teaching of English in the secondary schools have appeared so rapidly in the current decade that they seem to have shot up apart from any history of teaching the subject. This of course has not happened. The word *development* implies a continuum. No competent English teacher would speak to students about any age, period, or milieu in literature — even of a so-called *avant garde* literary milieu — as though it had emerged with a *tabula rasa,* bringing nothing, owing nothing.

And so it is with the emerging English curriculum. Instructed bv its experience in the schools and by new knowledge and new ideas, the English program has always emerged upward and outward, progressing, enlarging itself with new experience. The growth of English as a subject has never been gradual or steady. There have been times when English has seemed to leap ahead, settle down, even reverse itself in reaction to new directions. In the schools and out of the schools, English has had good environments and poor environments, good advice and poor advice. For evidence of this fact, one has only to visit old books on the teaching of English, which in many college library stacks remain in a kind of purgatory, where they are occasionally blessed or damned by doctoral candidates in search of background information for their dissertations.

In the chapter which follows, the European and early-American heredity of English as a subject, the birth of English in American secondary schools, the early growth and later development in the schools, and the recent emergence of English as a new questioning spirit (characterized by a new restlessness and a desire for identity) will be viewed as part of the mainstream. Constantly asking questions about itself, English today is attempting to define itself and find its own way in an age which is producing many kindred spirits in the curriculum of the secondary schools.

Definitely not an exhaustive history of the teaching of English in American secondary schools, this chapter attempts to establish only an outline or possibly a case history up to 1960, so that new developments can be seen with more perspective.

AN ANTI-ENGLISH HEREDITY

When the founders of America came to these shores, they came to establish new freedoms for themselves; but they also came with English traditions, practices, ethics, and the institutions to perpetuate their way of life. In imitation of the grammar schools of England, the early colonists organized secondary education around Latin grammar schools. These schools were dominated by the religious teaching in the colonies and by the academic spirit and aims of the first universities, whose chief aim was to prepare clergymen. Books chosen for adolescents were of classical Greek and Latin vintage and were read as models in the practice of these languages. Since the aim of the Latin schools was college preparation, a statement such as the following by Harvard College dictated not only the books to be included on the secondary level, but the manner in which they were to be studied:

> When any scholar is able to understand Tully or such like classical Latin author *extempore*, and make and speak true Latin in verse and prose *suo ut auint marte;* and decline perfectly the paradigms of nouns and verbs in the Greek tongue, let him then and not before be capable of admission into the college.[1]

[1]John Franklin Brown, *The American High School* (New York: The Macmillan Company, 1917), p. 13, quoting from "New England First Fruits," in *Old South Leaflets,* No. 51, p. 2.

So rooted were the classical languages in the Harvard curriculum that scholars could "under no consideration use their mother tongue within the limits of the college, unless summoned to deliver in English an oration or some other public exercise."[2] Yale College maintained a similar ban until 1774.

In view of this great stress on proficiency in the classical languages in imitation of English universities, it is understandable that books selected for reading in American preparatory schools served almost exclusively as models for an exhaustive drill in these languages. Statements by the grammar school preparatory for William and Mary College made the placement and use of books at the secondary level very clear.

> Let the Latin and Greek Tongues be well taught. We assign Four Years to Latin, and two to the Greek. As for Rudiments and Grammars, the Classick Authors of each Tongue, let them teach the same books, by which Law or Custom are used in the schools of England. Nevertheless, we allow the schoolmaster the liberty, if he has any observations on the Latin or Greek Grammars, or any of the authors that are taught in his school, that with the Approbation of the President, he may dictate them to the Scholars. Let the Master take special Care, that if the Author is never so well approved on other Accounts, he teach no such Part of him to his Scholars, because nothing contributes so much to the Learning of Languages as dayly Dialogues, and familiar Speaking together, in the Language they are learning; let the Master therefore, take Care that out of the Colloquies of Corderius and Erasmus and Others, who have employed their Labours this way, the Scholars may learn aptly to express their Meaning to each other.[3]

Excluded from any serious study or use in preparatory schools and colleges, English was taught at home or in a "dame school" conducted by a housewife in her home.

THE BIRTH OF ENGLISH AS A SUBJECT

Academic and religious dissent gave birth to English as a subject, first in England and later in America. Driven from their

[2]Charles Carpenter Fries, James Holly Hanford, and Harrison Ross Steeves, *The Teaching of Literature* (New York: Silver Burdett and Company, 1926), p. 19, quoting *Statuta Harvardini,* 13, 1642, 1655, 1685.

[3]Elmer Ellsworth Brown, *The Making of Our Middle Schools* (New York: Longmans, Green, and Co., 1905), p. 130, quoting from the *Charter and Statutes of the College of William and Mary.*

es by the Act of Uniformity in 1667, determined English ——hen organized boarding schools and introduced subjects which related more, as they claimed, to the practical aspects of life. A very early announcement of formal instruction in English grammar in America seems to have carried a like conviction. The following advertisement appeared in the *South Carolina Gazette* on November 16, 1734:

> William Waterland of Wassamacaw School . . . gives notice that any Gentleman Planter or others, who want to send their Children to School, may be provided with good con-veniency for boarding. . . . . Writing and Arithmetic in all its most useful Parts, and the Rudiments of Grammar are taught, but more particularly English, of which great care is taken, and by such methods as few Masters care to take the Trouble of, being taught Grammatically.

In like spirit, Benjamin Franklin established Franklin's Phila-delphia Academy in 1751 with three departments: Latin, English, and Mathematics. With the addition of English composition in Franklin's Academy came the inclusion of certain approved books by English authors to serve as models. This marked the first serious study of certain English classics in the curricula of American secondary schools.

Although the admission of English classics marked a change, it caused little or no change in the way in which literature was taught; Milton's *Paradise Lost,* Pope's "Essay on Man," and Cowper's "Task" were generally used for sentence parsing, oral reading, and declamation. Finally, the early emphasis on English literature in Franklin's Academy diminished in favor of Latin and Greek classics, and in 1771 English grammar was the only English offering in the curriculum.

In carrying this summary of grammar instruction into the nineteenth century, three points should be noted: (1) attention to English grammar as a prescriptive school subject increased until its prestige almost paralleled that formerly enjoyed by the grammars of classical languages; (2) colleges and universities did not give much attention to the study of English grammar; (3) a few grammarians — influenced toward the end of the century by findings in anthropology, psychology, phonetics, and historical-comparative philology — began moving away from the formal, deductive analysis of English grammar toward a scientific analysis based upon inductive observation and classification; (4) as the century came to a close, grammar in the schools was not greatly influenced by any rejections of formalism or by the lack of attention to grammar in the colleges.

Early course descriptions reveal that English grammar was subsumed under composition, which was often fragmented into separate courses in orthography, word analysis, sentence analysis, and punctuation. This way of defining composition set up a barrier to progress in the teaching of writing which continues to the present day. Thus fragmented, composition could not take guidance from rhetoric or be a unified course or an articulated sequence of courses.

DOMINATION AND REFORM

Influenced by the unyielding entrance requirements of such institutions as Harvard and Yale, which finally accepted English studies, the secondary schools took serious note of the English classics stressed in college entrance examinations. Observe the Harvard requirement for the academic year 1873-74:

> *English Composition.* Each candidate will be required to write a short English composition, correct in spelling, punctuation, grammar, and expression, the subject to be taken from such works of standard authors as shall be announced from time to time. The subject for 1874 will be taken from one of the following works: Shakespeare's Tempest, Julius Caesar, and Merchant of Venice; Goldsmith's Vicar of Wakefield; Scott's Ivanhoe, and Lay of the Last Minstrel.[4]

Especially alarming to secondary teachers was the stress on written examinations. Before 1870, secondary school students did little more than recite and translate Greek and Latin. There was little reason for change, because this procedure was followed in college classes. Now, in the face of increasing enrollments, colleges were turning to lectures and written examinations. Secondary schools had to try to develop skills in writing.

[4]U. S. Bureau of Education, *Reorganization of English in Secondary Schools,* Bulletin No. 2. Compiled by James Fleming Hosic (Washington, D.C.: U. S. Government Printing Office, 1917), p. 12, quoting from *Twenty Years of School and College English,* Appendix.

SOME STARTLING SUGGESTIONS

The statement by Harvard was not as startling as those made by the Conference on English, which was organized by the Committee of Ten[5] and met at Vassar College in 1892. Turning to the high schools, the Conference recommended that English be "pursued" for "five hours a week during the course of four years." Three of the five hours were allotted to the study of "good authors" and certain masterpieces, as opposed to "a manual of literary history"; two hours a week were allotted to composition for the first two years and one hour for the last two years. Emphasizing some history of the English language, some knowledge of the sound system and of the word structures of English, vocabulary study, dialects and literary language, usage, the decay of inflections, and changes in the meaning of words, the Conference left one hour a week in the fourth year, during which "historical and systematic" grammar could be "assigned."

In many respects, the Conference reflected the hard work of persons with vision. One might have supposed at this time that domination by the colleges had been broken and that a "new" English curriculum had emerged for the secondary schools. This of course was not the case.

EARLY DISPUTES IN LITERATURE

Conservatives were also hard at work. In 1894 the New England Commission of Colleges and the New England Association of Colleges and Preparatory Schools were invited to send delegates to a conference with the Middle States committee in Philadelphia. The National Conference on Uniform Entrance Requirements in English was formed at this meeting, marking the beginning of a long tradition.

But reaction came very soon. Acting under pressure from the National Education Association, the National Conference on Uniform Entrance Requirements adopted in 1895 an "open list" which allowed candidates for admission to college some freedom of choice in books offered for the examination. Western colleges

[5]"Report of the Committee of Ten on Secondary School Studies, With Papers Relating Thereto," Chapter 2, *Report of the Commissioner of Education* for the Year 1892-93, II (Washington, D.C.: U. S. Government Printing Office, 1895), 1415-1495.

responded first. Eastern colleges were slower to allow any change in prescribed lists, and for many years criticized the latitude offered by western colleges.

The first volume of *The English Journal* clearly illustrates the conflict between preparatory schools and technical high schools and between eastern colleges and western colleges in the matter of teaching certain selections of literature in high school. Mr. D. O. S. Lowell of the Roxbury Latin School defended the reading of prescribed selections by all students on the grounds that it would be unnatural, undemocratic, and unjust to do otherwise. Mr. Samuel Thurber, Jr., of the Newton Technical High School, reacted to Mr. Lowell's case for the classics by saying that

> Sixteen year old boys who cannot follow the story of *Ivanhoe,* or of *A Tale of Two Cities,* but who like rather well *Swiss Family Robinson* and *Tanglewood Tales* are going to give trouble when they come to Macaulay, Burke, Milton, Ruskin and Tennyson. True it is that the teacher of English must live by faith and hope. To trust blindly, however, that a boy has in some way got something good into his system from studying a book which he does not understand, and which bores him unutterably, is not any form of optimism; it is mere sentimentality.[6]

Such attacks, however, did not do much to weaken the position held by advocates of prescribed classics in the high school program as the century came to a close.

LATER DEVELOPMENT

THE MOST VEXING PROBLEM

The most vexing problem facing high schools at the turn of the century seemed to be that of determining best ways of establishing uniform college entrance requirements. To this end, the College Entrance Examination Board was established in 1900. A work listing all the questions in English set by the College Entrance Examination Board from 1901 through 1928 includes

---

[6]Quoted by Charles Swain Thomas in "The English Course in the High School: The New England View," *The English Journal,* I (January, 1912), 92. Reprinted by permission of the National Council of Teachers of English.

the following sources: *Lorna Doone, The Pilgrim's Progress, The Last of the Mohicans, Robinson Crusoe, Joan of Arc, David Copperfield, A Tale of Two Cities, Silas Marner, Cranford, The Vicar of Wakefield, The House of Seven Gables, Ivanhoe, Quentin Durward, Kidnapped, Treasure Island,* and *Henry Esmond.* Of these, the two which appeared most frequently were *Ivanhoe* and *Silas Marner.*[7]

The National Conference on Uniform Requirements in English allowed some option in books read and even some choice in questions to be answered on examinations. The Conference also "sedulously avoided the appearance of dictating the high school course in English and did not suggest any definite organization of subject matter," but it issued a list of "recommendations" in 1897 that at least suggested ways to organize instruction. Its importance in this case history of English as a subject is that the following recommendations pertaining to literature pointed the way for changes:

That the prescribed books be regarded as a basis for such wider courses in English study as the schools may arrange for themselves.

That a certain amount of outside reading, chiefly of poetry, fiction, biography, and history, be encouraged through the entire course.

That each of the books prescribed for study be taught with reference to:

   a. The language, including the meaning of words and sentences, the important qualities of style, and the important allusions;
   b. The plan of the work, i.e., its structure and method;
   c. The place of the work in literary history, the circumstances of its production, and the life of the author.

That all details be studied not as ends in themselves, but as means to a comprehension of the whole.

NEEDED RESEARCH ON READING INTERESTS

In the midst of departure and conservatism, there was some much-needed research. The first studies that put literature taught

[7]Edna Hays, *College Entrance Requirements in English: Their Effects on the High Schools,* Teachers College, Columbia University Contributions to Education, No. 675 (New York: Bureau of Publications, Teachers College, Columbia University, 1936), pp. 1-76.

in American high schools to a test were surveys asking students to rank selections in the order of their liking for them or their opinion of their value. The first study of this type with any scope was done during the first semester of 1910-11 and involved 5,803 students in 209 classes in the Illinois system.[8] Reactions received totaled 21,684. Although results cannot be listed here, it is interesting to note selections given positions at extreme ends of the list. *A Tale of Two Cities, Silas Marner,* and *Macbeth* ranked at the top; Chaucer's works, Franklin's *Autobiography,* "The Deserted Village," "The Rime of the Ancient Mariner," and Emerson's *Essays* ranked at the bottom. Typical of most surveys of interests which followed, this study reflected only students' feelings of likes and dislikes toward the selections.

Crow, however, went beyond most studies of interest by asking students to make value judgments on seventy-four classics assumed by the researcher to be valuable as "means for the realization of certain social ends."[9] This researcher contended that "to young readers people are just people until they find such books as *Peter Sterling, The Making of an American, Silas Marner.*"[10]

Studies of reading interest did much to focus research on specific factors assumed to affect the interest, appreciation, and meaning students take to and get from their reading of literature. Irion's research into factors affecting comprehension is one of the most intensive and extensive of such studies. After conducting his study of the ability of students to comprehend literature usually offered at the ninth grade level, Irion concluded that literary comprehension correlates "to a considerable degree" with intelligence and with reading comprehension, and "that it is very hazardous to assume that ninth grade students can comprehend the usual literary diet by simply reading."[11] He also concluded that the sexes do not appear to differ in ability to com-

[8]Charles Maxwell McConn, "High School Students' Rankings of English Classics," *The English Journal,* I (May, 1912), 263.

[9]Charles S. Crow, *Evaluation of English Literature in the High School,* Teachers College, Columbia University Contributions to Education, No. 141 (New York: Bureau of Publications, Teachers College, Columbia University, 1924), p. 7.

[10]*Ibid.,* p. 10.

[11]Theodore W. H. Irion, *Comprehension Difficulties of Ninth Grade Students in the Study of Literature,* Teachers College, Columbia University Contributions to Education, No. 189 (New York: Bureau of Publications, Teachers College, Columbia University, 1925), pp. 71-72.

prehend literature. This last conclusion might seem to disagree with the findings of Crow earlier and of Norvell later, but Crow and Norvell were interested more in the attitudes, feelings, and interests behind literary choice than in the matter of comprehension stressed by Irion.

The results of Irion's study received reinforcement in 1927 from the more comprehensive research of Mary Crowell Burch. Burch sought to determine whether many selections read in high school were on a difficulty level suitable for students in the high school grades. Conclusions reached by the researcher are:

> Much of the present course of study in high schools is suited to the ability of about 25 percent of the members of each class.
>
> Some method must be used to determine the difficulty value for a given group of any piece of literature which is being considered for a place in the course of study.
>
> The relation of the difficulty value of the selection to the range in difficulty of satisfying reading is an important factor determining its inclusion in the course if it is to lead to a voluntary choosing of material of the same sort and a development of reading interests.[12]

THE "HOSIC REPORT"

While the forces of tradition were continuing the emphasis on a few English classics well into the twentieth century, revolts against tradition were gathering strength. Probably the first really effective effort to reform the English curriculum was made through the "Hosic Report," which was issued in 1917 by the National Education Association and the National Council of Teachers and entitled *Reorganization of English in Secondary Schools.*

Declaring that the "entire doctrine of 'preparation' for higher institutions is fallacious," and indicating that the emphasis in 1899 on college preparation had prevented the Committee of Ten from making a realistic high school English program possible, the "Hosic Report" stressed relating items of knowledge to the experience of adolescents.

Directed by cultural, vocational, social, and ethical aims, the

[12]Mary Crowell Burch, "Determination of a Content of the Course in Literature of a Suitable Difficulty for Junior and Senior High School Students," *Genetic Psychology Monographs,* IV (August-September, 1928), 288-89.

report stressed "command of the art of communication in spee
and in writing," and thoughtful reading leading to taste in t..
independent selection of books. Contributing committees focused
on composition, literature, oral expression, business English,
general reading, the library, and administrative problems.

The committee on composition stressed "the development of
the expressional powers of the individual pupil . . . rather than the
teaching of specific form and rules." Grammar was placed under
composition, and its "functional" aim was to improve speaking,
writing, and reading. "In general, the grammar worth teaching is
the grammar of use — function of the sentence — and the grammar
to be passed over is the grammar of classification — pigeonholing
by definition."

The committee on literature presented an interesting blend of
liberalism and conformity. First, it stated that all literature which
does not contain a "natural appeal" for pupils "should be excluded, no matter how respectable it may be from age or reputa-
tion." On the other hand, the committee expressed the belief
that if a classic doesn't appeal to a "healthy-minded" student,
the choice of book isn't at fault; the teacher is "unable to point
the way." For terminal students and those in industrial and
vocational schools, the committee even suggested "books not
truly deserving the name of literature," but only as means to an
end — that end being "literature broad in its humanity, and rich
and full in its spiritual appeal."

One year after the "Hosic Report," another step was taken in
an effort to shift from the traditional emphasis upon subject
matter mastery to a greater emphasis on preparing students for
contemporary society. Through offering seven "Cardinal Principles" as guidelines in secondary education — health, command of
fundamental processes, worthy home membership, vocation,
citizenship, worthy use of leisure, and ethical character — the
Commission on the Reorganization of Secondary Education
reflected a growing national concern, that of providing the soaring
high school population with an educational program that would
meet the needs of all. Realizing such a goal necessitated a shift
from emphasizing college preparation, with its intensive study of
a few English classics, to preparing all students for efficient living
in a democracy — no matter what their vocational or professional
aims might be.

A New Curriculum Emerges

Influenced by the philosophy of such men as John Dewey, Boyd H. Bode, and William H. Kilpatrick, and by the expanding range of students in the high schools, the National Council of Teachers of English approved in November 1929 a proposal to direct its president, Ruth Mary Weeks, to create a curriculum commission. After several months of organization, a commission was formed with Wilbur W. Hatfield, Council Secretary, as Chairman. Six years later, this commission issued its report, *An Experience Curriculum in English,* with the primary objective of providing through the language arts those experiences for adolescents that would help them to develop the power of self-direction they would need to cope successfully with the modern age of rapid industrial, social, and economic change.[13]

The complete "pattern curriculum" in *An Experience Curriculum in English* offered interrelated "experience strands" and teaching units for kindergarten through grade twelve under the following major phases of English: literature, reading, creative expression, communication (both oral and written), and corrective work.

Stressing individual and group reading of literature, freedom of selection for students, and flexibility in placing selection on any grade level, the publication concluded that "the experiences through literature are the ultimate objective. The author's sensory and social experiences, his imaginings, and his feelings, are what he has tried to put into his writing, and they are what the reader wishes to get." Elsewhere the report stressed that "the intrinsic worth of such experiences is the only valid reason for the reading of literature."

Under such headings as Informational Reading, Reflective Reading, Problem Reading, Reading for Report, and Reference Reading, units were offered which gave many English teachers their first look at their responsibilities in developing skills needed by students in reading non-literary materials. Under Creative Expression, guidelines were established for relating composition and literature. The development of sense-reactions to nature and

[13]*An Experience Curriculum in English,* A Report of a Commission of the National Council of Teachers of English, W. Wilbur Hatfield, Chairman (New York: D. Appleton-Century Company, 1935), Preface, p. ix. Reprinted by permission of the National Council of Teachers of English.

to the objective world; the sharpening of observation of people; a sensitivity to details of form, color, rhythm, symmetry, balance, proportion; and the discerning of sound rhythm in musical arts were among the objectives.

Speech experiences in this curriculum included social conversation, telephone conservation, interviews and conferences, discussion, questions and answers, organizations, special occasional speeches. Writing experiences included social letters, business letters, news stories, reports, opinions. Under Instrumental Grammar, units were presented on such immediate objectives as "To secure consciseness by using infinitives as adjective and adverbial modifiers." Corrective Teaching included usage, spelling, corrective work in reading, and corrective work in speech. An interesting forward-looking addition is an elective course in grammar by which "students should be led to observe the facts of language as heard in speech and found in writing, and should make inductions and generalizations from the facts."

The fact that *An Experience Curriculum in English* listed objectives and materials in the way often described in teaching units caused it to be an even greater stimulus for English teachers. In an effort to record many of the plans subsequently tried by teachers, the National Council of Teachers of English compiled narrative accounts, outlines, unit assignment sheets, notes on experience-centered curriculum studies, courses of study, and critical suggestions from 274 English teachers over a period of four years. This publication was named *Conducting Experiences in English.*[14] Through these numerous narrative accounts, one can see that teachers on a continuum from traditional to radical tried to adjust their programs to the philosophy that literature is the written expression of the ideas and emotions caused by man's reaction to life. Grammar, which was taught to improve students' written expression, was given a minor role.

NEEDED RESEARCH IN THE TEACHING OF LITERATURE

Many changes in the English program during the twenties and the thirties stimulated research into the different ways of organiz-

---

[14]*Conducting Experiences in English,* A Report of a Committee of the National Council of Teachers of English, Angela M. Broening, Chairman (New York: D. Appleton-Century Company, 1939).

ing literature instruction. The study possibly most deserving of mention here seems to be the one conducted by Coryell to evaluate extensive and intensive teaching of literature in the eleventh grade. The extensive method is defined as "the rapid reading of a comparatively large amount of literature with general comments and discussions in class," and the intensive method is defined as "the detailed, analytical study of the minimum of literature required."[15] Although the test results lead the researcher to conclude that students taught by either method did equally well in comprehension of material read, the reactions and responses of the students lead her to conclude that the extensive method caused more enthusiasm among students and resulted in a "deeper, wider, and more satisfying experience." It is also interesting to note that students of low ability did significantly better in reading ability and in oral expression after the extensive approach than after the intensive approach. This study offered some proof to teachers that they did not have to depend upon an intensive study of a few selections as the best approach to the comprehension of literature.

INTEREST IN THE "MOTHER TONGUE"

The twenties and thirties also witnessed some interest in the study of the English language. World War I had made the nation aware of at least four language problems: (1) the low level of literacy of men called into service, (2) differences in dialect and levels of usage, (3) the need for clear, concise, accurate communication, and (4) the need to use the full power and resources of language in persuasion. These matters led to a noticeable rise of attention to the vernacular or "mother tongue" of the nation, with particular attention paid to the spoken language. Semantics received some attention, but it made no great impression on the schools.

Although the growing attention to the "mother tongue" was at first little more than a "functional" effort to produce error-free English, scholars began making strong pleas for scientific in-

---

[15]Nancy G. Coryell, *An Evaluation of Extensive and Intensive Teaching of Literature,* Teachers College, Columbia University Contributions to Education, No. 275 (New York: Bureau of Publications, Teachers College, Columbia University, 1927), p. 1.

vestigations of American English. (In his presidential address before the National Council of Teachers of English (1928), Charles C. Fries insisted that there was no one criterion of good speech, but rather levels of "dialect" observed at various social levels. He asked for a shift of emphasis away from the study of rules in the schools to accurate investigations of language practices, but his forward-looking plea caused no greater impact on grammar teaching than did radical-looking grammar revisions by Otto Jespersen and Janet Rankin Aiken.

NEEDED RESEARCH IN USAGE

Fries' comments looked ahead to the "usage movement," which was awakened by the research of Sterling A. Leonard in 1932 and Albert H. Marckwardt and Fred Walcott in 1938. Both studies, published as monographs by the National Council of Teachers of English, were extensive surveys with results tabulated and analyzed statistically.[16] The first submitted 230 expressions "of whose standing there might be some question" to 229 judges "composed of thirty linguistic specialists, an equal number of editors, twenty-two authors, nineteen business men, and about 130 teachers of English and of speech." These judges rated 71 of the test expressions as acceptable, 38 as illiterate, and the remaining 121 as in doubt, with no consensus. Marckwardt and Walcott took Leonard's 230 expressions to such impressive judges as the *Oxford English Dictionary, Webster's New International Dictionary,* and several leading grammar and usage books. The researchers found that as judges these sources were not as conservative as Leonard's live authorities. After stating that their "analysis should dispose once and for all of the journalistic cry of heresy and radicalism so frequently raised against the Leonard report," Marckwardt and Walcott guessed that "a survey of fact rather than of opinion would, in all probability, have increased the number of established usages from a meager seventy-one to 177." Although these reports did not revolutionize the teaching of grammar and usage in the schools,

[16]The studies are: Sterling A. Leonard, *Current English Usage,* National Council of Teachers of English, English Monograph No. 1 (Chicago: Inland Press, 1932); Albert H. Marckwardt and Fred G. Walcott, *Facts about Current English Usage,* National Council of Teachers of English, English Monograph No. 7 (New York: D. Appleton-Century Company, 1938).

they caused progress in at least two respects: (1) English teachers became more aware of the importance of live scientific observation and description of the spoken language, and (2) textbooks began to show some linguistic liberalism.

MORE DISPUTES IN LITERATURE

Changes in literature, as indicated earlier, were viewed with much more concern than those in language. So sharp were the controversies that leaders in English education were prompted to help teachers seek a middle ground in the interest of effective teaching. The early debate over whether an intensive study of selected books or a free reading assignment was better caused Helene Hartley to suggest a *via media* through "intensive study and free reading integrated to one end—the development of power to read books as the basis of all pleasure in reading and on any true appreciation of literature."[17] A few years later, Dora V. Smith attempted to convince many English teachers, through replying to one, that a middle ground could be found amid the sociological emphasis of liberal methods, and that teachers could preserve their sound scholarship.[18]

It was against such a background of controversy that Smith delivered her presidential message before the Boston convention of the National Council of Teachers of English, November 26, 1936. After opening her speech by saying, "It is a wholesome experience to be teaching English when all the world questions what we are doing and why we are doing it,"[19] she made one of the most effective pleas for "bridge" or transition novels that can be found in the professional literature:

The difficulty is that at the moment when they think *Tarzan of the Apes* the greatest book ever written, we give them *Silas Marner,* and we wonder why it doesn't take. I would not for one moment suggest the abandonment of the one for the other. I would argue only for a sane bridging of that gap, for the filling of our courses of study during the

[17]Helene W. Hartley, "A Via Media in the Teaching of Literature," *The English Journal,* XXI (April, 1932), 298.

[18]Dora V. Smith, "Seeking a Middle Ground," *The English Journal,* XXVI (June, 1937), 446.

[19]Dora V. Smith, "American Youth and English," *The English Journal,* XXVI (February, 1937), 99.

ninth and tenth grades with wholesome stories of adventure in far-distant lands. I should map the adventure areas of the world to show that the jungle and Arizona have no monopoly on courage. Then I should gradually inject into the picture the bravery of the microbe hunters, stories of moral courage, of victory over forces less obvious and less easily combatted, hoping that by this process I should ultimately lead some of my pupils — not all of them, I know in advance — to an appreciation of *Silas Marner* and similar novels of great spiritual achievement. Whenever a literary classic meets any one of these needs, I should take it off its shelf of literary loneliness and let it compete on its own merits with those companions of the trail which boys and girls choose because they want to choose them and freely enjoy. It is a task of the teacher to guide to higher and higher levels.[20]

ANOTHER CURRICULUM EMERGES

While *Conducting Experiences in English* was being compiled, the National Council of Teachers of English published a monograph that asked teachers to broaden their plans. In "project" methods ranging from structured to unplanned and incidental correlations, teachers were urged to draw upon all subject matter — even readings in Greek and Latin — "to deal with the student as a dynamic whole . . . in the midst of genuine living, posing problems of immediate significance to himself, and devising and using means for their solution."[21]

Attempts at unstructured correlation carried many problems. For example, it was reported that incidental correlation (occurring spontaneously in the classroom) could involve students in projects that were being conducted in other subjects, and that factors of greatest importance might be missed completely as discussions and activities stemmed mainly from the particular interests of the teacher and the students.

As controversial as many procedures may have been, it should be added here that many teachers realized the limitations of their experiments and did these things in the faith that ways could be found to teach literature more successfully. The method of teach-

[20]*Ibid.*, pp. 108-9. Reprinted by permission of the National Council of Teachers of English.

[21]*A Correlated Curriculum,* A Report of the Committee on Correlation of the National Council of Teachers of English, Ruth Mary Weeks, Chairman (New York: D. Appleton-Century Company, 1936), p. 4.

ing by literary types (stressing the novel, short story, poem, etc.) had been the most common approach to organization, but now other ways could be tried. One departure, for example, was illustrated in *A Correlated Curriculum* with "A Character Training Unit" which included such topics as school life, ethical attitudes, character in conflict, the power to influence, and the nature of achievement. In effect, this was an attempt to organize literature instruction thematically.

LITERATURE AND THE ADOLESCENT

Contemporary with *A Correlated Curriculum* and *Conducting Experiences in English* was *Literature as Exploration,* a book that spoke directly and honestly to all English teachers with an understanding that went to the very core of literature instruction — whether it was organized by types, experience, theme, or by any other method. The following statement is typical of its insight:

> No matter what the form — poem, novel, drama, biography, essay — literature makes alive and comprehensible to us the myriad ways in which human beings meet the infinite possibilities that life offers. And always in books, we seek some close contact with a mind uttering its sense of life.[22]

Stressing that a teacher's choice of books must have "relevance to the general emotional level of his students and to the possible points of stress in their particular home or community background," Rosenblatt added that an intensive study of difficult words and syntax is not the solution. By the time the students have some grasp of the language, she continued, they will have lost interest in the work. The author acknowledged that a classic that "presents experiences and ideas highly relevant to the student's own preoccupations" can stimulate enough interest to overcome the language barrier, but she observed that too often the classics are introduced to students who are too young to "feel in any personal way the problems of conflicts treated." In summary, "difficulties in understanding . . . are usually not a mat-

[22]From *Literature as Exploration,* by Louise M. Rosenblatt, pp. 6-7. Copyright, 1938, by D. Appleton-Century Company. Reprinted by permission of Appleton-Century-Crofts, Division of Meredith Publishing Company.

ter of words and syntax, for words must be apprehended in some context of experience."[23]

A SEARCH FOR IDENTITY

The Forties: The War and Social Studies

Through most of the forties, the greatest single influence on curriculum change in English was, of course, World War II. In step with the total effort in these war years, the Basic Aim Committee of the National Council of Teachers of English attempted to set several directions in literature selection and instruction. One was that literature should be drawn from all ages to "develop a keen sense of permanent social values."[24] As such, it was not to be a "storehouse unrelated to the problems with which the world grapples today."[25] Another direction was that American literature should receive more emphasis than the literature from all other nations. A third aim was that literature from all periods in history and from all nations, should be suited to the needs and capacities of adolescents. At least three main goals were implied: (1) to take a realistic and objective look at all time-honored selections; (2) to select and use the kind of acceptable transition literature mentioned earlier by such leaders as Smith, LaBrant, and Rosenblatt; and (3) to teach all literature related to the needs and capacities of adolescents in a way that would bring out its greatest potentials for the students taught.

In the middle of the pressures of correlated programs and experienced-centered programs, and of sociological, patriotic, psychological emphases at the beginning of World War II, many English teachers became confused. Witness the following statement:

> Surely while we assume this colossal role, the "thing" we all thought we meant by English (I shall let the reader define it) has little chance. Any minute now, I expect English-as-

[23]*Ibid.*, p. 256.
[24]Basic Aims Committee of the National Council of Teachers of English, "Basic Aims for English Instruction in American Schools," *The English Journal,* XXXI (January, 1942), 45.
[25]*Ibid.*, p. 46.

new-world-order to be our next assignment — or possible English-as-combating-paganism![26]

And close to the end of the war another teacher wrote that "there is a movement now under way to absorb the English curriculum within the field of social science — a movement which seems to be gaining momentum."[27] In attempting to establish their identity, English teachers stressed that the English teacher, not the social studies teacher, was better equipped to give the student an aesthetic experience and an "inner regeneration" as he came to understand the meaning of his heritage. For evidence of this belief, one has only to scan articles written for *The English Journal* during these years. English teachers had become quite fearful that subject-matter integration, especially with social emphases, would weaken the teaching of English skills.

These articles were written more from a fear of the future than of the present. Actually, integrated or "core" programs were not common in the secondary schools during the forties. An investigation conducted by the United States Office of Education and published in 1949 reveals that of the nation's 24,000 secondary schools, only 3.5 per cent or 833 schools had adopted an integrated or "common learnings" method of instruction.[28] It is true, however, that nine-tenths of the "core" programs in existence had formed by combining the once separate subjects of English and social studies. And the report does tend to support teachers' predictions, for it indicates that the trend toward combining English and social studies seemed to be increasing.

The Fifties: Literature for Adolescents

As the teaching of English moved into the fifties, several trends became noticeable. In their attempts to focus more squarely on the concerns and needs of adolescents through

[26]George H. Henry, "Is English on the Way Out?" *The English Journal,* XXXI (April, 1942), 288.

[27]Charles I. Glicksberg, "In Defense of English," *The English Journal,* XXXIV (June, 1945), 309.

[28]Grace W. Wright, *Core Curriculum in the Public High Schools An Inquiry into Practices, 1949,* Bulletin No. 5, Federal Security Agency (Washington, D.C.: U. S. Office of Education, 1950), p. 28.

literature study, English teachers had loosened their hold on the adult classics as the only material to aid students in their reading of novels. Some teachers selected novels on different levels of difficulty and included them with the classics. These were generally selected to relate to a theme or topic of immediate interest and concern to the students. Literature study became less concerned with the lives of authors, facts, and technique analysis, and more concerned with having each student find through books ideas that had meaning in terms of his own life. Under these influences, even the popular "types" approach to organization had changed from knowing specific books to gaining important understandings about life. Thematic and "types" approaches sometimes involved the use of reading ladders and reading designs that moved the student a step at a time—not with one book but a selection of books—to novels on high levels of difficulty and maturity. As Dora V. Smith pointed out in 1951, "There is little place in high school teaching today for the old approach to the 'novel' by having every pupil read the same book at a set pace of 35 pages a day."[29]

The thematic approach to organizing literature study was given impetus in two books published by the Commission on the English Curriculum of the National Council of Teachers of English. The first volume, *The English Language Arts* (1952), commended English teachers for selecting and using books that stressed social and personal values, and it urged them to learn more about the intellectual capacities and the emotional and intellectual maturity that adolescents take to their books. Volume III, *The English Language Arts in the Secondary School* (1956), established the Council's philosophy by heading one chapter "Meeting Youth's Needs through Literature." In noting the sharp differences among adolescents within a single classroom, the chapter stressed the "necessity of furnishing, in classroom and library, reading materials paralleling in difficulty the range of ability among the members of the class." Reaching the problem of prescribed lists, the chapter stressed instead the importance of giving students experience in choosing books so they will act with more independence and thought in making

---

[29]Dora V. Smith, "How Literature Is Taught in the Secondary Schools of Today," *NEA Journal*, XL (April, 1951), 286.

choices of books later in life. The intensive and extensive study of literature formed no dualism in the chapter; within the framework of idea-centered topical units such as "Back-Country America," and through the adjustment of the "types" approach to include books suited to the needs of individual students, both intensive and extensive reading were included.

In 1950, Norvell published an extensive and influential study of students' reading interests. It included 50,000 children and 625 teachers. And, in addition to providing the usual rankings by choice, it included the results of related research on the following factors to see to what extent they should be considered by the teacher in selecting literature for students: sex, age or maturity, intelligence, special interests (adventure, humor, etc.), the classroom situation, the teaching methods used, and the community influences. The researcher concluded that age, intelligence, and a "good" teacher are not significant factors in selecting literature for students.[30] On the other hand, he concluded that sex of the reader and special interests are highly significant factors. Norvell also concluded that students prefer individualized reading to reading or study in common.

Studies were also made on the development of literary appreciation, and on the development of behavior change and maturity through literature. The main observation to be made about these, too, is that they were student-centered rather than subject-matter centered. In fact, a shift from a controlling interest in historical facts, biographical facts, and literary facts to an increased interest in ideas and values seems to be central to change in literature instruction in the fifties. Prominent in this trend were doctoral studies on such topics as the responses of adolescents to literature written to evoke sympathy; the responses of adolescents to literature containing certain experiences of personal development; the assumptions concerning human experience underlying selected literature for adolescents; the effect of literature on the radical attitudes of eleventh-grade students. This trend might have gained prominence in the Sixties, but it seems to have been eclipsed by the rapid emergence of other influences which will be described in Chapter 2.

[30]George W. Norvell, *The Reading Interests of Young People* (Boston: D. C. Heath and Company, 1950), pp. 5-6.

What Is American English?

Language study also underwent some very significant changes in the forties and fifties. Influenced by Jespersen, Fries, Leonard, and Marckwardt and Walcott, the profession continued its interest in gathering accurate and reliable information about the English language.

In the schools some enlightenment produced a little flexibility, but more prevalent was the increased interest in eliminating specific errors. Added attention to specifics caused differences of opinion between "experts" and teachers and created the immediate need for accurate and reliable information concerning English usage. In answer to this plea, the National Council of Teachers of English commissioned Charles Fries to gather facts for a "preliminary sketch of the inflections and syntax of American English with especial reference to social class differences." This he did in his book *American English Grammar* (1940).

With the help of the Modern Language Association of America and the support of the Linguistic Society of America, Fries obtained files of informal correspondence in the possession of the United States Government. These files contained letters written by Americans with widely divergent backgrounds. Basing his investigation not upon prevailing conclusions about errors in writing but upon a careful examination of word forms, function words, and syntax in the correspondence, Fries discovered that the major characteristic of the writing of persons with limited schooling was their very limited, conservative, and restrictive use of the resources of their language. They simply did not seem aware of the many possibilities available in the use of language. The most striking difference between the language of this group and that of educated writers was not in word forms commonly classified as "errors," but in the "poverty-stricken" language of the uneducated as opposed to the varied and fairly rich language of the educated.

Fries' data led him to urge teachers to base their teaching on "an accurate description of the actual practices of informal Standard English," to "stimulate among our pupils observation of actual usage," and "to go so far as possible in giving them a practical equipment for this purpose."

In a later book, *The Structure of English* (1952), Fries described a grammatical system based upon his scientific observation and analysis of recorded and transcribed American English conversation. More than any other source, this book aroused the interest of the profession, even of many practicing classroom teachers, in descriptive linguistics. A new spirit emerged, and with it came an increased desire to really answer the question, "What *is* the American English language?"

A New Grammar

In 1956 two textbooks on descriptive linguistics appeared: Harold Whitehall's *Structural Essentials of English*, which was used as a college text in structural linguistics, and Paul Roberts' *Patterns of English*, which was designed as a high school text. Soon, a small number of English professors began teaching structural linguistics to future high school English teachers as though it had become the final word on English grammar. Many experienced English teachers snorted. Student teachers returned to campus believing that they had been misguided in college and had simply not learned anything useful about English grammar. In these troubled times, college professors did not win many converts in the high schools.

Another New Grammar

It was not long before English teachers were informed that their new grammar was not the only new grammar. First in the work of Noam Chomsky and later in *English Sentences* (1962), a high school text by Paul Roberts, English teachers were asked to consider the merits of transformational-generative grammar. Going beyond the basic patterns described by structural grammar, transformational-generative grammar describes a process for "generating" new sentences from "kernel groups" or basic patterns. The big question in the minds of many teachers soon became, "Which English grammar should I teach?"

Which Grammar Is Best?

Teachers have moved into the present decade of the sixties with some words of caution about which grammar to teach. J. N. Hook, H. A. Gleason, and other leaders in language and the teaching of language, have suggested that a wise teacher should choose from the new grammars information which seems most promising and most accurate in informing students about the language. Hook and Gleason have further stressed that no linguist or secondary English teacher is in any position to condemn or dismiss any system or to declare that it is the best one for the high school curriculum.[31] This is at least timely advice, for there exists today the possibility that a teacher may be rather narrowly informed, even in an English institute taught by a leading linguist or grammarian. A high school teacher who feels converted or greatly relieved after a brief introduction to what he may assume to be *the* new English grammar (either structural or generative) may spend too much time the following year attempting to teach all that he thinks he has picked up.

THE LANGUAGE SPECTRUM

More beneficial to students than the current attention to the several English grammars may be the growing attention to the broad spectrum of language and language study. Teachers are beginning to give serious attention to the history of the language, etymology, and semantics against the broad backgrounds of verbal behavior and communication theory. Also receiving more attention are the various levels of usage and the dialects which characterize changing spoken American English and enrich and diversify the language. The effort is to intrigue students with language, and to make them aware of its power, richness, versatility, and cultural implications. Through conducting their own investigations of language and language problems, students might become more relaxed with their language and have a greater respect for it. The general aim in language study appears to be shifting from an elimination of specific "errors," in spite of a greater focus on upward social mobility, to a study of *how* persons with various backgrounds communicate in the society. Such matters will be discussed in greater detail in Chapter 5.

* * *

[31]It should be noted, however, that specialists in English education seem to be placing more hope in transformational-generative grammar than in structural linguistics.

The following chapters will outline current theories, practices, and attitudes which have special implications for the teaching of English today and tomorrow. Referring mainly to developments which have become most apparent during the late fifties and early sixties, the discussions will include new efforts to classify and structure knowledge so that it might be taught more effectively. Discussions will also include the teaching of new knowledge and new structures for subject matter in light of new structures for the teaching method. Literature, composition, and language will be discussed from this point of view; and whenever it seems appropriate in the interests of students in the secondary schools, comments will be made about their individual growth in knowledge and use of English.

Against the background of recent trends in teaching the subject, such developments as the following will be mentioned: (1) current teaching tools and aids, including programed materials, transitional and pioneering textbooks, paperbacks, units and kits of multilevel materials developed for individualized, self-instruction, greater use of all the mass media, transparencies and tape recorders in teaching composition, tapes for oral pattern practice in usage and dialect; (2) current methods for designing the curriculum, including patterns for individualized instruction within classes, team teaching, humanities classes, flexible scheduling, and nongraded classes.

Two closely related topics will receive very serious attention. Because English teachers and researchers in the teaching of English do not have adequate instruments of measurement to use in assessing the changes which they now expect in students, the need for a new look at tests and measurements will be stressed. Because new developments in English have come quickly at a time when there is an unprecedented shortage of English teachers, needs and trends in the preparation and continuing education of English teachers will be given close scrutiny.

SELECTED REFERENCES

Applebee, Roger K. "National Study of High School English Programs: A Record of English Teaching Today." *The English Journal,* LV (March, 1966), 273-81.

Carpenter, Charles. *History of American Schoolbooks*. Philadelphia: University of Pennsylvania Press, 1963.

Commission on the English Curriculum, NCTE. *Summary Report of English Curriculum Study and Development Centers Funded by the Program in English of The U.S. Office of Education*. Champaign, Illinois: National Council of Teachers of English, 1966.

Fallon, Bernie (ed.). *Educational Innovation in the United States*. Bloomington, Indiana: Phi Delta Kappa, 1966.

Frazier, Alexander (ed.). *Ends and Issues: 1965-1966: Points of Decision in the Development of the English Curriculum*. Champaign, Illinois: National Council of Teachers of English, 1966.

Gleason, H. A. "English Grammars," *Linguistics and English Grammar* Chapter 4. New York: Holt, Rinehart and Winston, Inc., 1965. Pp. 67-87.

Hook, J. N. "Grammar(s): A Rationale, *"The Teaching of High School English,* Chapter 9. New York: The Ronald Press, 1967. Pp. 270-318.

Jewett, Arno. *English Language Arts in American High Schools*. U. S. Office of Education, Bulletin No. 13. Washington D. C.: U. S. Government Printing Office, 1959.

Jewett, Arno. "National Trends in Teaching of English." *The English Journal,* XLVI (September, 1957), 326-29.

Keppel, Francis. *The Necessary Revolution in American Education*. New York: Harper & Row, 1966.

LaBrant, Lou. "As of Now." *The English Journal,* XLVIII (September, 1959), 295-303.

Leonard, Sterling A. *Current English Usage*. National Council of Teachers of English, English Monograph No. 1. Chicago: Inland Press, 1932.

Marckwardt, Albert H., and Fred G. Walcott. *Facts about Current English Usage*. National Council of Teachers of English, English Monograph No. 7. New York: D. Appleton-ton-Century Company, 1938.

Mersand, Joseph. "The Emerging English Curriculum of the 1960's." In *Concepts of English: 1964: Traditions and Innovations*. Report of the Fourteenth Annual English Conference of the Metropolitan Detroit Bureau of School Studies. Edited by Myron Simon. Detroit: Metropolitan

Detroit Bureau of School Studies, Wayne State University, 1964. Pp. 1-12.

Morrison, Samuel Eliot. *The Intellectual Life of Colonial New England.* Ithaca: Great Seals Books, A Division of Cornell University Press, 1956.

National Association of Secondary School Principals. "The Emerging Curriculum in English in the Secondary School." *Bulletin of the National Association of Secondary-School Principals,* XXX (February, 1946).

Radner, Sanford. *Fifty Years of English Teaching: A Historical Analysis of the Presidential Addresses of NCTE.* Champaign, Illinois: The National Council of Teachers of English, 1960.

Shugrue, Michael F. *New Materials for the Teaching of English: The English Program of the USOE.* Publications of The Modern Language Association of America, (September, 1966), (Preprint). No. 4, Vol. LXXXI, New York: The Modern Language Association of America, 1966.

Smith, Dora V. "Reestablishing Guidelines for the English Curriculum," *The English Journal,* XLVII (September, 1958), 317-26, 338.

Squire, James R. "English at the Crossroads: The National Interest Report Plus Eighteen." *The English Journal,* LI (September, 1962), 381-92.

――――. "National Study of High School English Programs: A School for All Seasons." *The English Journal,* LV (March, 1966), 282-90.

Tate, Gary, ed. *Reflections on High School English.* NDEA Institute Lectures 1965. Tulsa: The University of Tulsa, 1966.

II

The New Method

When the prospective English teacher of even fifteen years ago took a methods course, he learned a series of steps or procedures which he could follow to insure maximum learning in his classroom. In all likelihood, he learned how to apply the teaching steps outlined by Herbart in the nineteenth century: motivation as achieved by presentation of materials in such a way as to prepare the learner's mind for reception of new knowledge; association of materials by comparison to give the learner an idea of what he has to comprehend; synthesis and supplementation of new materials; and application of knowledge gained to exercises and illustrations. To help him manipulate the learning experience effectively, the prospective teacher was carefully prepared to handle routine classroom matters. He learned how to make lesson plans, sociograms, and seating charts; he learned how to structure groups, seating arrangements, and conferences; and he learned how to give tests and grades, and how to build up the confidence of his students. The methods course emphasized how to teach, while the question of what to teach was left primarily to curriculum makers and textbook publishers. The teacher who emerged from this training was expected to be able to take the procedures and techniques he had learned and impose them on any subject matter with acceptable results.

Since the major educational aims of the time were social rather than intellectual, the dominance of method over material was natural. Schools were supposed to produce people with healthy personalities — people equipped with the skills, attitudes, and values needed to get along with others. Among the basic skills which students needed most were those included in the term *language arts*: reading, writing, speaking, and listening. English was a tool subject, and English teachers diligently sought the most effective ways to teach those tools.

Toward that end, the Commission on the English Curriculum of the National Council of Teachers of English produced its 1952 volume, *The English Language Arts*.[1] The Commission endorsed the teaching of English as a tool subject and, armed with the latest research findings on transfer of training, insisted that the "social, emotional, and intellectual situation in which a language skill is developed should be as identical as possible with the situations in which it is to be used in life outside of school."[2] The Commission also identified broad areas of student needs, experiences, and interests around which instruction should be centered. Units such as "Life Is What We Make It" and "Making the Most of Oneself" were suggested for tenth grade; "The Struggle for Freedom" and "What Shall We Make of America?" for eleventh; and "Problems of Vocation" and "Success, Its Meaning and Sources" for twelfth.[3]

The third volume of the NCTE's curriculum series, *The English Language Arts in the Secondary School,*[4] published in 1956, departed slightly from the emphasis on the teaching of English as a tool subject using methods determined by the needs, interests and abilities of the learner. The departure is evident in the Commission's statement that what teachers need is some means of organizing instruction "that implements the principles of learning through use in purposeful activities and at the same time recognizes the relatedness of all the language skills and literature."[5] The development of healthy personalities was still recognized as the main goal of instruction, but the notion was beginning to grow that the methods employed in reaching that goal somehow had to be related to the unique characteristics of

[1]The Commission on the English Curriculum of the NCTE, *The English Language Arts,* Vol. I (New York: Appleton-Century-Crofts, Inc., 1952).

[2]*Ibid.,* p. 34.

[3]*Ibid.,* pp. 135-38.

[4]Commission on the English Curriculum of the NCTE, *The English Language Arts in the Secondary School,* Vol. III (New York: Appleton-Century-Crofts, Inc., 1956).

[5]*Ibid.,* p. 69.

English as a discipline. The Commission, therefore, endo
the unit method of teaching for most of the language arts, ̇ʊ̇ʟ̇
recognizing the aesthetic dimension of literature, advocated wide
independent reading for enjoyment. The result was that literature,
at last, no longer had to be taught as a means to social adjustment
or as a tool for gaining proficiency or insight into some other
academic area: the nature of literature itself could determine the
ends and means of its study.

BEGINNINGS OF THE NEW METHOD

The appearance of Volume III was only one of a series of
events which occurred in the late 1950's to herald the beginning
of a new approach to the teaching of English. One of the most
important of those events, Russia's launching of Sputnik, resulted
in a comprehensive reappraisal of American schools. The teaching of English, no less than science, came under close scrutiny.
Prompted by the criticism of men such as Rickover, Bestor,
Flesch, and Conant, the American public demanded to know
what the schools were doing and how they proposed to meet the
challenge to the national security. Something more than social
adjustment was being demanded, and nothing less than acceler-
ated pursuit of knowledge toward more practical ends would be
accepted.

Educators were accused of coddling the nation's youth, of not
making the most of students' abilities, and of not filling the school
day with good, hard work. Response to the criticism was quick
and decisive. New and more difficult tasks and materials were
added to courses of study at all grade levels. In English, literature
and accompanying writing activities once reserved for college
work were moved down to the high school level, and those once
taught in high school were pushed down to junior high school.
Faced with the task of teaching skills which many of their
students were not ready to master, English teachers were forced
to change their teaching methods. Former methods of motivation,
presentation, and evaluation proved inadequate to meet the new
demands for excellence in English.

Questions concerning what really constitutes excellence in
English immediately began to arise, and those questions prompted

another event which had far-reaching effects. Throughout 1958, a group of twenty-eight national leaders in the teaching of English, representing the American Studies Association, the College English Association, the Modern Language Association of America, and the National Council of Teachers of English, held a series of meetings supported by the Ford Foundation for the purpose of re-examining the whole problem of the teaching of English. The result was a statement of thirty-five basic issues facing English teachers.[6] Beginning with the assumption that English is not merely a group of skills underlying the rest of the school's curriculum, but that it has a subject matter of its own, the participants asked questions designed to discover what that subject matter properly consisted of, how it could be articulated, how it should be taught, and who should be responsible for all phases of student and teacher preparation. Few, if any, answers came out of the meetings, but the questions which were asked added momentum to at least one piece of advice: look to English itself for answers.

The event which seemed to crystallize the answers to the questions which everyone was asking at the time was the publication of Jerome Bruner's *The Process of Education*.[7] In a book of less than a hundred pages, Bruner provided answers to hundreds of questions. His thesis was simple: every subject has its unique structure and the easiest and most effective way to learn a subject is to grasp its structure. The structure of a subject, according to Bruner, is the relationship that exists between the parts and the whole. Learning the structure of a subject allows other things to be related to it. Teaching structure, Bruner insisted, would, in fact, promote transfer of learning.

As to how, when, and to whom structure should be taught, Bruner cast aside many old notions. Forcing all students to go through lock-step analytic processes is a waste of time, he said. Material should be presented inductively in order to encourage students to take intuitive leaps. The discovery of a subject's structure should begin with the student's first encounter with it,

---

[6]Committee of the American Studies Association, the College English Association, the Modern Language Association, and National Council of Teachers of English, *The Basic Issues in the Teaching of English* (Ford Foundation, 1958).

[7]Jerome S. Bruner, *The Process of Education* (Cambridge: Harvard University Press, 1960). See also: Jerome S. Brunner. *Toward a Theory of Instruction*. Cambridge: The Belknap Press of Harvard University Press, 1966.

since any concept that is worth teaching can be taught at any level. Slow students, as well as bright ones, should be directed to the continual search for structure, and interest in the search per se should be the prime motivating force. The challenge, Bruner insisted, is for scholars and educators in every field to identify the structure of their discipline so that the constant recurring relationships can be taught to students at all levels.

DESCRIPTION OF THE NEW METHOD

English scholars and teachers took up Bruner's challenge, and in the process of attempting to discover the structure of their subject, they brought about what must be considered the most significant development in the teaching of English today—a completely new concept of method. The new method is that process of investigation which is demanded by the subject under study. It is sometimes inductive, sometimes deductive. It is sometimes invention, sometimes discovery. It is sometimes carried out individually, sometimes in small groups, and sometimes in large groups. It is sometimes teacher-led, sometimes not. It is sometimes lengthy, sometimes not. And it is sometimes predictable, sometimes not. The new method is, however, always new, for every subject is unique.

The new method differs from the old method in at least two significant ways. First, the old method began with a prescription of procedures and techniques; the new method begins with a description of what to teach. Second, the old method tended to be geared to the immediate interests, needs, and abilities of the learner; the new method is geared to the characteristics of the material or skill to be learned.

What was once called teaching method is largely what is today called curriculum design. In most schools an attempt is made to provide for interests, needs, and abilities by putting students in the proper track. College-bound students of high ability are grouped together, as are groups of other students with different abilities and aspirations. The problem of evaluation is solved in some schools by specifying the range of grades which can be given in each track. By demanding prerequisites and corequisites, schools attempt to provide for learning readiness and vertical as well as horizontal continuity of learning as a matter of curriculum design. As the shortcomings of those attempts to provide for individual learning differences through multiple tracking systems become more obvious, a trend toward building into the curriculum some time for independent individual study appears to be developing. There can be little doubt that the modern curriculum is, indeed, a design for learning in which the teacher has a highly specialized role not as a manipulator of students but as a dispenser of information about his subject matter.

NEW ROLE OF THE TEACHER

The new teacher, therefore, must, above all, be a scholar in his field of specialization. He must know the past and present developments in his subject and be prepared to make intelligent guesses about the future. [For the English teacher, this means that he must know the history of the English language, how it has changed, and what changes it is apt to undergo in a changing world where old patterns and media of communication are becoming obsolete. He must be familiar with his literary heritage and his literary horizon, both national and international. His familiarity must include the literature of the new media as well as the old. Also, he must be a master of the processes of oral and written composition. Finally, the English teacher must be familiar with new and old materials that are available for him to use to teach his subject. More than ever before, the new English teacher, perhaps because of the changing views of his role and the nature of his task, will have more freedom to choose from the great bulk of available materials those which seem to him best suited to teaching the structure of his subject.

The new teacher often finds that the specific objectives of the courses he teaches are determined for him. There is, as a matter of fact, a growing trend toward careful, long-range articulation of the English program from kindergarten through high school. But within the limits of that program, today's teacher has considerable freedom in selecting those materials and activities which he thinks can most profitably be used to meet those objectives.

He chooses his materials and activities with the course objectives in mind, and having chosen them, he must analyze them for clues as to how they should be taught. Given the characteristics of the material or the skill to be taught and knowledge of the materials and skills taught earlier, he decides how the study should proceed. Is the material structured in a simple, straightforward manner so that the students can read it on their own and inductively come to an understanding of it, or is it material which demands a lot of background information that is best provided by a lecture? Is the skill in question one which, like writing, depends on individual work, or is it one which, like reading poetry orally, demands an audience? Sometimes several possible procedures are suggested by the area under study, and he may choose the one which has the greatest appeal to the students. But the new teacher, using the new method, considers the subject first.

Today the focus of study in English methods classes is on the subject itself. One of the most popular methods texts of the day, Hans Guth's *English Today and Tomorrow*,[8] has been criticized because of its lack of depth in teaching technique. Guth's book, however, is very much in keeping with the new method and the English teacher's new role because his emphasis throughout is on content and the teacher's responsibility for knowing, evaluating, and using that content effectively to develop competence in the use of language. The nature of language itself, not the nature of the learner, is clearly what Guth insists that the English teacher must be most concerned with.

FUTURE OF THE NEW METHOD

Most English teachers and scholars are too happy with the new method to push for any kind of change. English is their first love, and the new method allows them to indulge themselves. And there can be little argument that the place to look for clues to structure, sequence, and method is content. Form and content are one, even in the structure of teaching. Through the application of the new method teachers will probably come to a greater understanding of the basic processes and structures of their discipline

[8]Hans P. Guth, *English Today and Tomorrow* (Englewood Cliffs, N.J.: Prentice-Hall, Inc., 1964).

than ever before. With that understanding will come the possibility of making their students' study of language a richer, more rewarding experience.

But if that is to happen, a new dimension must be added to the new method – a concern for the structure of the student. The first products of the new method, today's high school graduates, are asking, "So what?" They have studied English intensively, and they know much about it. Yet, they haven't been touched by it. It doesn't mean anything to them because it was taught as if the meaning were inherent in the subject, as if all they had to do was to study English and the meaning of it would come to them naturally. It didn't, and it won't until teachers realize that the structure of language study must fit into the structure of the learner.

Little is known about the learner's structure. True, researchers have found and labeled various dimensions of it – intelligence, cognitive style, value system, level of aspiration, level of anxiety, etc. – but they know very little about how those dimensions are related in the total personality structure. Without this knowledge of the learner's structure, teachers will be greatly handicapped in their efforts to help the student to see how knowledge about the structure of English subject matter can be meaningful to him.

This lack of knowledge should not force teachers back to a narrowly-defined student-centered curriculum. The process-structure-centered curriculum appears to hold the greatest promise for the future, but that promise will probably not be realized until teachers are convinced that the students, not they, give meaning to what they teach.

III

Literature
and the New Method

There can be little doubt that the teaching of literature, more than any other area of language study, has been revolutionized by the new method. The time when literature was taught mainly for its sociological and historical values is past. It is becoming less common to find literature still selected, organized, and taught primarily as a means of gaining insight into life and its problems. Today, literature is taught chiefly as means of gaining insight into literature itself.

EACH SELECTION COMPLETE AND UNIQUE

The most common approach is to teach each piece of literature as a work, *sui generis*. The assumption is that every piece of literature — novel, poem, play, short story — has its own structure, its own unique combination of elements that give it unity and distinguish it from every other work of its kind. Teachers are, of course, interested in having their students recognize those elements that are common to the various genres and those elements that distinguish literature from non-literature, but they seem to feel that the best way to achieve that recognition is to teach individual selections intensively and to rely on later generalizations as a means of making such distinctions.

The method of inquiry is usually inductive, that is, teachers direct their students to note particulars and then encourage them to generalize and to hypothesize about the relationships among the particulars and the whole. Since the emphasis is on seeing the parts in relationship to the whole, intensive analysis is usually delayed until students have read the entire work. The usual procedure is to require a quick reading of the entire work first, in order to establish the whole. Teachers have discovered, however, that with some of the longer pieces of literature they have to teach and with some of their slower and less motivated students, that it is impractical to delay discussion until a first reading has been accomplished. Frequently, therefore, they rely on their own summaries or various audio-visual presentations of the work, such as films, film strips, and records to set the framework for close analysis of the text.

When a first reading of the text is required, teachers often supply their students with study guides which direct the reading by focusing attention on significant elements and relationships. The study guides usually consist of questions to be answered as the text is read, but sometimes they simply call the student's attention to something he needs to notice. Study guides occasionally even include biographical information about the writer and historical information needed to understand the language, customs, and events depicted in the work. In keeping with the New Criticism, though, historical and biographical information is seldom given, the assumption being that a good piece of literature contains within itself all that is needed to understand it.

THE QUESTIONING PROCEDURE

Once the whole has been established, the inquiry proceeds with a series of questions designed to lead the students to a discovery of the work's structure and to a judgment of its literary merit. Although each piece of literature is considered unique, the questions asked about any piece of literature are frequently the same. Teachers feel that asking the same questions is an excellent way, as a matter of fact, of emphasizing differences among selections by noting how the answers differ.

The Commission on English of the College Entrance Examination Board recently listed the following questions as ones that should form the basis of literary inquiry:[1]

I. Questions about the text itself
  A. Questions of form
    1. What is its kind?
    2. What are its parts?
    3. How are the parts related?
  B. Questions of rhetoric
    1. Who is speaking?
    2. What is the occasion?
    3. Who is the audience?
  C. Questions about meaning
    1. What meaning has each work in its particular context?
    2. What do the diction and grammar of the text tell about its purpose?
    3. What is the paraphrasable content of the work, its "statement"?
    4. What intention—high seriousness, irony, comedy, and the like—is apparent and how is it made apparent?
    5. What part of meaning is sacrificed by paraphrase, by substitution of words other than those used by the author?
II. Questions of value
  A. Questions about personal response
  B. Questions of excellence

The Commission's questions are obviously intended to lead a student to the discovery of a work's structure, but it is interesting to note that what the Commission considers structure conflicts with what many literary scholars consider to be structure.

STRUCTURE AS EXTERNAL FORM

To the Commission, and probably to most English teachers today, the structure of a piece of literature is its external form, the

[1]Commission on English of the College Entrance Examination Board, *Freedom and Discipline in English* (New York: College Entrance Examination Board, 1965), p. 58. Reprinted by permission of the Commission on English of the College Entrance Examination Board.

mold into which a writer pours his ideas and experiences. Thus, there is the structure of a short story, of a drama, of a poem, of a novel, etc. According to this view, structure is what distinguishes one form of literature from another. Although a writer may occasionally modify the structure he has chosen to work with by adding a new element or changing a characteristic of the form, he usually is limited to establishing new relationships among the elements common to all works of that genre. New relationships affect the work's meaning, not its structure.

In a classroom where structure is thus conceived, the student's job is, first, one of identification and classification. He must know the parts of the various genres and be able to identify them in a new context, the work he is studying. Once he has done that, he must decide how the parts are related, that is, how one affects the other. Only then is he asked to talk about the meaning of a selection and to evaluate it in terms of others of its kind and in terms of his personal response to it. The student is usually taught that a piece of literature has a single meaning which is inherent in the work itself and that thorough knowledge of the work as an object created by a writer for a purpose is essential to the understanding of that meaning.

STRUCTURE AS RECURRENT THEME

To another group of scholars, the structure of literature seems to rest in its meaning, or at least its recurrent themes. The assumption is that all literature is concerned with basic humanistic relationships between man and God, man and nature, man and other men, and man and his inner self. Though those themes may be expressed in various modes (romantic, comic, tragic, or ironic) and in various forms (plays, poems, short stories), they constitute the essence, or structure, of literature. Literature dealing with the same theme has essentially the same structure.

The student must know enough about the characteristics of literary genres and possible modes of expression to be able to determine with accuracy which of the basic themes constitutes the structure of a piece of literature. His is the job of seeing that content can take many forms by discovering that any piece of writing which claims to be literature deals in some way with the same content — the human condition. His study proceeds from an understanding of the particular elements in a single work to an understanding of common elements in various genres, modes, and themes. Throughout, he is engaged in the process of comparing and contrasting the piece under investigation with every other piece of literature he has read.

STRUCTURE AS MATRIX

There is still another group of scholars who contend that the structure of literature is its skeleton, the matrix of relationships that hold it together and give it unity. To the degree that a work has unity it has structure, and that unity is achieved not only through form but through content, also. In *Understanding Fiction,* Brooks and Warren equate structure with form and define it as "the arrangement of various elements in a work of literature; the organization of various materials (ideas, images, characters, setting, and the like) to give a single effect." Further, they say, "Form is not to be thought of as a sort of container for the story; it is, rather, the total principle of organization and affects every aspect of the composition."[2]

The key word in this concept of structure is "arrangement." Structure does not rest in the parts but in their relationships to each other and to the whole. Some attempts have been made to identify relationships that are used repeatedly in literature to give unity, such as comparison, contrast, and expansion, but none has succeeded in providing a comprehensive list of all the possible structural relationships found in literature. Rather than finally deriving a list which would cover every piece of literature, the emphasis is on discovering those relationships which can be found in a particular work without generalizing from them.

The student in search of this kind of structure must be able to identify all the elements in a work as well as their relatedness. In a short story, for instance, he must be able to identify and understand the characters, plot, setting, theme, symbols, author's choice of words, rising action, tone, mood, etc. and be able to

[2]From *Understanding Fiction,* p. 684, by Cleanth Brooks and Robert Penn Warren, Second Edition, Copyright © 1959 by Appleton-Century-Crofts, Inc. Reprinted by permission of Appleton-Century-Crofts, Division of Meredith Publishing Company.

relate each of those elements to the others. His goal must be to account for everything in the story as the author intended it. If he cannot do this, he can say that he either doesn't understand enough about the story, or that the piece doesn't have unity. His study is different from the others mentioned previously in that his focus is not on the formal or thematic elements themselves, but on the bonds that hold them together. His goal is not to isolate or classify parts or their characteristics, but to understand them as they relate to a particular context.

STRUCTURE AS LITERARY EXPERIENCE

There is still another view of structure which is influencing the teaching of literature today — namely, that structure exists in the interaction between a reader and the work of literature, in the literary experience. The proper study, according to this view, is the structure of the whole reading experience. One of the leading proponents of this view is Paul Goodman who states in *The Structure of Literature,* "Therefore, let us start from the art work as we experience it and find the working parts in what actually claims our attention."[3] The "working parts" cannot be named in advance of the reading, and they may not be the same for any two readers.

The reader's task is to try to understand what is happening to him as he reads and to discover what there is in the literature that is responsible for both the kind and the quality of the experience he has with it. Goodman and others argue that appreciation of the literary experience is enriched by an understanding of what affected it. Good writers, it is assumed, can force the reader to attend to what he otherwise would not notice and can, therefore, control in large measure the structure of the experience. Because of the experiences the reader brings with him to a work, what happens in the interaction may not be what the writer intended, if indeed he intended anything, and that is to be expected. The important thing is that, whatever the experience, the reader be able to understand it.

---

[3]Paul Goodman, *The Structure of Literature* (Chicago: University of Chicago Press, 1954), p. 16.

The significance of this view of structure for the student is that it makes him a collaborator in the work of art and frees him from having to account for everything in the work. He need only account for what he attends to. More than that, he doesn't have to begin with a naming of parts. What he begins with is the complete experience, his experience. His experience is neither good nor bad; it is simply his experience which no one else can duplicate exactly. He does not have to classify according to theme, mode or form; he does not have to be limited to the context of the work; and he does not have to get the precise message the writer intended. Still, he might do all of those things, depending on the structure of his experience.

CURRENT POPULARITY OF VIEWS

As indicated previously, the concept of structure as external form, a kind of receptacle, is the one most literature teachers hold today. The other concepts, particularly those based on recurrent relationships and themes, are gaining in popularity, but many teachers, probably because genre study is easier to organize, prefer to teach the concept which stresses characteristic forms. And nearly all teachers, probably because those three concepts are based on a greater degree of objectivity and therefore more easily evaluated, prefer them over the idea of experiential structure. They grant, of course, that what a student takes to a book affects his understanding and appreciation of it, but they generally believe that the object of literary study is to understand the work on its own terms.

Teachers have great faith in the notion that understanding leads to appreciation, or at least increases the base of appreciation. Aesthetics, like everything else, has become a science. To investigate, to know, is to appreciate. Few teachers today would begin a discussion of a piece of literature by asking his students if they liked or enjoyed it; most would reserve those questions until they were sure that understanding had been achieved. Even then, students are asked to document their opinions with references to the text. Literature study may have reached the point where art is no longer studied for art's sake, but for science's.

ORGANIZATION OF INSTRUCTION

The unit—the grouping of materials and activities around a topic or theme—is still one of the most popular devices for organizing instruction in literature because of its versatility and flexibility. Units can be adapted to the study of genres, themes, single works, historical periods, and cultural movements. The length of units, usually two to four weeks, facilitates periodic evaluation of progress and provides for the periodic changes of focus which are considered necessary to keep students interested. Objections to units are usually concerned with the focus of particular units rather than the unit idea itself. Whatever the focus, though, the unit has the advantage of providing either for the intensive study of some element common to several pieces of literature, or for the intensive study of a single work. It also provides the framework for bringing together the varied activities and materials needed to deal with differences in the interest and ability of individual students.

ORGANIZATION AND ANTHOLOGIES

Division of the literature course into units may or may not be the result of a teacher's planning. More often than not, it is the idea of the writers or publishers of literature anthologies. There is no doubt that the type of organization a teacher finds in the anthology he is given to teach is the most significant factor in determining how the course will be organized. The new method to the contrary, seldom does a teacher disregard the groupings he finds in anthologies in favor of his own. Fairness to publishers demands that it be said, however, that they make a concerted attempt to give teachers what they want. Teachers order books, and they influence what publishers make available for them to order.

Until recently, units based on chronology and cultural epochs were the most common type of units included in anthologies, particularly those in American and English literature. With the new method and the emphasis on structure, however, units based on the study of genres are becoming very popular. As suggested previously, the emphasis in studying literature today is on gaining insight into the formal characteristics of literature itself. Short stories, essays, poems, biographies, and other forms are being grouped together in anthologies as a means of studying form — its characteristics and development. An attempt is being made to group short stories, for instance, which demonstrate individually a particular characteristic of the short story form. One may be a story which depends mainly on plot development for its impact while another relies mainly on characterization or mood.

Units based on the study of genres are even beginning to replace thematic units in junior high school, and this development is characteristic of the present trend to move rigorous study of form downward through the grades. Theme-centered units focusing on social or personal interests and problems suggest sugar-coating to many teachers. Even in junior high school, they contend, a student should be taught to develop an intrinsic interest in literature, per se. They take support from Bruner's notion that a concept can be taught on many levels. How far this movement will go is difficult to say, but the trend is unmistakable. Other objections to thematic units are that too often the concentration on theme overshadows or eliminates consideration of literary merit and that inferior literature is often included for study simply because it contributes to the theme of the unit. Teachers are insisting on teaching good literature, and they want their student to know why it is good structurally.

TEACHING SINGLE WORKS

The insistence on good literature is perhaps one of the reasons for the increasing number of units being taught today with the focus on a single piece of literature. It takes a period of weeks to lead a class through the kind of intensive study of a long work which the new method demands. Within the framework of a unit, carried out over a period of weeks, every dimension of literary study can be explored.

The availability of paperbacks has also given impetus to this trend. Few of the new anthologies include novels. Rather, they offer study guides and suggest appropriate novels for a particular grade. As a matter of fact, the intensive study of several complete pieces of literature has replaced the anthology in many classrooms. Many teachers feel that the advantages to be gained from in-depth study of a few works are greater than those provided by a frequently cursory reading of a large number of selections.

INDIVIDUALIZED READING PRACTICES

Teachers are not willing to sacrifice scope for depth entirely, and they provide for scope by encouraging wide independent reading. Sometimes the independent reading program is an appendage to the basic program, and sometimes it is an integral part of the basic in-school program. Providing for independent reading within the structure of the literature course is a common practice.

Some plans, such as the Rutgers Plan which is in operation in many large city schools, provide two days a week for individual reading. On those two days students meet in a large reading room stocked with several thousand titles and choose what they want to read. Usually they are required to keep a record of what they read, and during individual conferences with the teacher they may be required to discuss their reading.

Some groups of students at the University of Iowa Laboratory School are given sixteen weeks in independent reading time. During that period they are allowed to read whatever they wish to read, but they know they will be marked on the amount of reading they do, the quality of the books they read, and their understanding of what they read. Like the Rutgers Plan, the Iowa program has been highly successful.

While those two programs are not typical of what usually goes on in the schools, they do reflect the concern of teachers that their students read extensively as well as intensively and that students be given freedom to select at least some of the books they read. Far more typical of the actual practices is the traditional system in which students are required to read a certain number of books on a prescribed list outside of school and to report on them in the classroom.

SELECTION OF MATERIALS

Selection of literature to be taught in secondary schools is based on several criteria: availability, level of difficulty, appropriateness to focus of study, traditional grade placement, and the literary quality of the work. Other factors, such as the cultural background of a particular group of students, may at times play an important part in the selection of materials, but seldom do they override the criteria listed above.

Availability is obviously the most practical criterion since teachers can teach only that which is available. Prior to the paperback explosion, teachers were usually limited to what appeared between the covers of the anthologies they taught. Some English departments stocked sets of classics which teachers could use to supplement the anthologies, and many departments still carry on that practice. Conflicting schedules and deadlines, however, make floating book sets difficult to work with since the dates for beginning and ending work with them must be scheduled far in advance. Still, with the availability of relatively inexpensive paperbacks, departments can afford to stock more sets—sometimes even duplicate sets—for teachers to use, making scheduling easier. The low cost of paperbacks has contributed to the practice of requiring students to purchase their own copies of books, a practice which has the added advantage of making book-owners of students.

CRITERION OF DIFFICULTY

The level of difficulty of a book certainly must be considered in its selection. Students for whom a book is intended must be able to read it. A change appears to be occurring in the thinking about what constitutes a book's level of difficulty. Formerly, it was judged by the subject or theme as well as by the difficulty of the language as measured by the old readability formulas. Since Bruner published his idea that any concept worth teaching can be taught at any level, the importance of subject as a criterion has diminished. The importance of language difficulty as a criterion has also diminished. In dealing with a Shakespearean play, for instance, teachers supplement the reading with audio-visual presentations that help to overcome the language difficulty. Study guides appear to help in overcoming it, too. What seems to be replacing those two factors as the main criterion of selection is the complexity of the work's structure, as measured by the variety of elements contained in the work and the kind of relationships which exist among them. Thus, a novel like *Lord of the Flies* is more difficult than *Johnny Tremain* not because the theme or language is more difficult to understand, but because its structure is more complex.

APPROPRIATENESS AS CRITERION

Appropriateness to focus of study and traditional grade placement are closely related as criteria of selection. Certain topics or areas of study are frequently designated for specific grades. World literature is frequently studied in tenth grade, American literature in the eleventh, and English literature in the twelfth. And in junior high school, unit topics are frequently named for specific grades, vocations in ninth grade and interpersonal relationships in the eighth. When teachers are handed such limitations, they clearly must select their material accordingly. Many conflicts arise from the clash between traditional grade placement and the current trend to move works downward through the grades. *Julius Caesar,* once taught mainly in the tenth grade, is now being tried in the ninth. Given the new focus of literary study, old standards of appropriateness are becoming obsolete.

It is no longer appropriate, for instance, to teach literature simply because it is representative of a period or because it is the only one of a writer's works that publishers can get permission to anthologize. What is taught must be worthy of intensive study as a good piece of literature. That is what literature teachers are demanding. The literature must be appropriate mainly to the objectives of literature study today.

The criterion of appropriateness is responsible for the inclusion of more modern literature in the curriculum. The students' familiarity with the language, situations, and values contained in most modern literature makes it easier for them to grasp its structure. Teachers also find that modern literature often has more intrinsic appeal to students, an appeal which is often needed to motivate students who are not interested in the study of literature for its own sake. More non-fiction is also being included in the literature course because it is appropriate to the objectives of the course and the interests of students.

Current problems with censorship are partially the result of the primacy of appropriate quality and structure as the criterion for selection. Many pieces of literature which qualify for study on the basis of appropriate quality contain ideas, words, and situations which individuals and pressure groups find objectionable. Obscenity and political indoctrination are the most frequently made charges against books, but there is growing pressure to ban books which allegedly present an unfavorable image of a group of people, even if the image is sociologically and historically truthful. Many teachers and administrators used to run scared at the first sign of an objection, and many still do, but there is a growing tendency to justify selections that are appropriate to the objectives of the literature curriculum. *The Student's Right to Read,* an official statement by the National Council of Teachers of English, is evidence of that trend.

In the near future someone may begin to question the validity of the current objectives of the literature curriculum. Time may prove them to be inappropriate, but at present, literature is being taught with a rigor that would surprise high school graduates of ten years ago. The English curriculum is still literature-dominated; James Squire has confirmed this fact in his recent National Study of High School English Programs. But teachers now have greater faith that through the study of literary structure the student can gain insight not only into literature, but also into his own use of language.

SELECTED REFERENCES

Arms, George. "Poetry," ed. Lewis Leary. In *Contemporary Literary Scholarship.* New York: Appleton-Century-Crofts, Inc., 1958.

Bowden, William. "Teaching Structure in Shakespeare." *College English,* XXIII (1962), 525-31.

Brooks, Cleanth, and Robert Penn Warren. *Understanding Fiction.* Second Edition. New York: Appleton-Century-Crofts, Inc., 1959.

———. *Understanding Poetry.* New York: Holt, Rinehart and Winston, Inc., 1960.

Burton, Dwight. *Literature Study in the High Schools.* Revised Edition. New York: Holt, Rinehart and Winston, Inc., 1964.

Commission on English of the College Entrance Examination Board. *Freedom and Discipline in English.* New York: College Entrance Examination Board, 1965.

Early, Margaret. "Stages of Growth in Literary Appreciation." *The English Journal,* XLIX (1960), 161-67.

Goodman, Paul. *The Structure of Literature.* Chicago: University of Chicago Press, 1962.

Irmsher, William. "An Apology for Literature." *The English Journal,* LII (1963), 252-56.

Miles, Josephine. "Reading Poems." *The English Journal,* LII (1963), 157-64.

O'Neal, Robert, ed. *Teacher's Guide to World Literature for the High School.* Champaign, Illinois: National Council of Teachers of English, 1966.

Roseblatt, Louise. *Literature as Exploration.* New York: D. Appleton-Century-Crofts, 1938.

———. "Literature: The Reader's Role." *The English Journal,* XLIX (1960), 304-10.

Schuster, Edgar H. "Discovering Theme and Structure in the Novel." *The English Journal,* LII (1963), 535-44.

White, Helen C. "New Perspectives on Teaching Literature." *College English,* XXIII (1962), 433-36.

IV

Composition
and the New Method

For many years written composition was taught as an atomistic process, one of mastering separate skills in isolation and gradually putting them together to produce a composition, as if the whole were no more than the sum of its parts. Even having something to say was treated as a skill which could be learned by breaking a topic down into its component parts as in an outline.

Thus the teacher — or more frequently the authors of the particular composition text the teacher used — itemized composition skills and arranged them in a learning sequence based on their complexity as determined by the number and order of lexical or syntactic units involved. In the typical sequence, a student learned to spell, to capitalize, and to organize words, first in simple sentences and then in complex, compound, and complex-compound sentences. Then, as he learned to string words together to produce grammatical sentences, he also learned to string sentences together to produce paragraphs, and paragraphs to produce longer compositions. Throughout, ability to identify parts preceded ability to use them.

Few people were satisfied with the products of such a system. Rhetoric instructors in college complained that many of the students being sent to them from high school could write neither "correct" nor interesting prose, their most common complaint being that most of the writing they received was sterile. Employers of students who didn't go to college complained that the schools

turning out people who couldn't even spell or punctuate
:tly, much less write interesting letters. High school
teachers were acutely aware of the shortcomings of the process.
The amount of time they spent teaching composition did not
seem to be justified by the results they obtained. Writing was an
unpleasant chore for most students, and reading and correcting
themes was an unpleasant chore for most teachers. Almost all
teachers preferred to teach literature, with the result that composition was nearly eliminated from the curriculum.

RESEARCH IN COMPOSITION

General dissatisfaction with the results of traditional composition instruction has resulted in considerable research on the
subject. The most significant studies have been reported in the
NCTE's *Research in Written Composition*[1] and Blount's "Summary of Investigations Relating to the English Language Arts in
Secondary Education: 1965."[2] The total effect of the investigations to date has been to cast doubt on many of the standard
assumptions and practices. The teaching of traditional grammar
has consistently been shown to have little effect on the improvement of writing. The teaching of transformational and structural
grammars has also been shown to have little effect on writing,
although recent studies consistently show the study of transformational grammar to be effective in teaching sentence structure and variety. The method of theme correction used by the
teacher also has been shown to have little effect on improvement
of writing. None of the research has clearly demonstrated the
value of post-writing activities on either the part of the teacher or
the student as means of improving subsequent writing. Even
frequency of writing appears to have little effect on improvement
of composition. Weekly writing assignments appear to be no
more effective in improving writing ability than do monthly
assignments. Research has done little to suggest new practices

[1]NCTE Committee on the State of Knowledge about Composition, *Research
in Written Composition* (Champaign, Illinois: National Council of Teachers of
English, 1963).

[2]Nathan S. Blount, "Summary of Investigation Relating to the English Language Arts in Secondary Education: 1965," *The English Journal,* LV (May,
1966), 591-608.

to replace the old. Thus, one fact seems clear: new metho
teaching composition are needed.

EMERGING PRACTICES

Some new practices are already emerging, partially as a result of the research which has been done, but mostly as a result of the new method of carefully examining the content of written discourse itself for clues. Thus far, research has been useful in showing what doesn't improve one's ability to write. The job of identifying promising new practices will be left to English teachers and scholars working separately or as groups in such research projects as the curriculum study centers currently being sponsored by the U. S. Office of Education, several of which are devoted to the study of composition. The teaching of composition can be expected to change dramatically in the next several years as a result of the intensive investigations now being conducted, but a few trends are beginning to develop which may very well point in the direction of change.

One of the most pervasive trends is a return to the use of the term "rhetoric" for composition, a return which is much more than just the revival of an old name. Different from traditional rhetoric in several significant ways, the "New Rhetoric" or "Neo-Classical Rhetoric" stresses cooperation between the writer and reader in a search for truth. Harold Martin has called the new rhetoric "a way of coming to know as well as a way of communicating what is known . . . the principal means by which the educated man tries to discover and transmit the truth about himself and about the world as he understands it."[3] Gone is the old notion that rhetoric consists of a bag of tricks with which the writer or speaker persuades his audience to take his point of view. The new rhetoric is conceived as thought unfolding in the search of truth, however tentative. While traditional rhetoric was concerned with skill in expressing preconceived arguments and points of view, the new rhetoric is concerned with the exploration of ideas. While traditional rhetoric was based on established patterns of discourse, the new rhetoric is based on the

[3]Harold Martin, *The Logic and Rhetoric of Exposition* (New York: Holt, Rinehart & Winston, Inc., 1958), p. 4.

assumption that organization grows out of the subject being treated. The new rhetoric, in short, is based on the notion that the basic process of composition is discovery, not recovery. In the process of composing, the writer or speaker discovers what he really wants to say about a topic, and his effectiveness depends on his ability to communicate what he has learned to his audience.

COMPOSITION AND COMMUNICATION

The new rhetoric places great emphasis on purposeful and effective communication, and teachers are, more than ever before, teaching students what is involved in the communicative process. The role of the sender, the role of the receiver, the role of the medium, and the *gestalt* of the total situation are significant areas of concern. Students are being led to discover how the sender's experiences affect the form and content of the message he sends and how the receiver's experiences affect the way he decodes and interprets the message. Limitations imposed by the medium and the situation are relatively new concerns in the process of communication, but with the renewed concern for factors which affect communication they are given considerable attention in the new rhetoric.

With the new emphasis on communication, it follows that semantics and usage occupy a more central position in composition instruction than formerly, with grammar slowly leaving the spotlight. The native speaker's problems of communication are seldom the result of ungrammatical constructions. They more often result from poor choice of words for the situation or from failure to recognize the potential meanings of the symbols he uses. Students are learning that if they want to communicate effectively with their audience, if they want to be understood, they must choose their words carefully in terms of the idiom they employ and the meaning they intend. Levels of usage and abstraction are concepts which must be mastered in today's composition class.

Many teachers feel that the careful analysis of communication also improves ability to think logically. Teachers are demanding that what their students say and write make sense, that their conclusions follow from the evidence or argument presented.

Exercises in identifying assumptions and testing their validity are becoming common. The whole process of thought is demanding more attention, probably as a result of the emphasis on communication, but also as a result of recent studies which show that writing improvement follows practice in thinking a problem through. Composition teachers are not, of course, teaching courses in formal logic, but they are teaching the processes of induction and deduction and the difference between statements of fact and opinion. They are also teaching students to explore the relationships between language and thought and between the word and the thing it represents.

The logic of the sentence as a vehicle for generating thought is also receiving considerable attention. The old notion of the sentence as a group of words which express a complete thought has generally been abandoned in favor of a concept of the sentence as a group of words which represent progressive generation of an idea toward completion. Words in a sentence represent a tentative idea to be modified by limitation or expansion in subsequent sentences. Recent work by Francis Christensen has brought new insights to the logic of the sentence as a unit with several structural layers, all of which may contribute to the generation of ideas. Christensen's work shows that "the mere form of the sentence generates ideas. It serves the needs of both the writer and the reader, the writer by compelling him to examine his thought, the reader by letting him into the writer's thought."[4] In his latest work, Christensen has applied similar principles to the generative aspects of the paragraph.[5]

PREWRITING EMPHASIS

In keeping with the new rhetoric, teachers are putting more emphasis on preparation for writing as a means of helping students think through what they plan to write before putting it down on paper. The purpose is to help students collect, test, and sort their ideas and develop a strategy for presenting them.

[4]Francis Christensen, "A Generative Rhetoric of the Sentence," *College Composition and Communication,* XIV (October, 1963), 157.
[5]Francis Christensen, "A Generative Rhetoric of the Paragraph," *College Composition and Communication,* XVI (October, 1965), 144-757.

Before writing begins, the choice of words and selection of mode of expression are considered from the standpoint of purpose, audience, and effect. The student is led to adopt what Wayne Booth has called "the rhetorical stance." Having found a definition of his audience, his argument, and his tone of voice, the student is ready to write. He knows what he wants to say and how he must say it. His rhetorical stance helps him sort out his ideas, choose his words, organize his thoughts, and provide for the internal continuity demanded by the position he has taken.[6]

Similar to Booth's concern for rhetorical stance is Walker Gibson's concern for the writer's *voice*. Gibson stresses the importance of the writer's deciding upon the *voice* he is going to assume in his composition. Having decided upon the voice, or role, he wants to assume, the writer must then choose words, syntactic structures, arguments, examples, and tone consistent with that voice. The writer's voice must in a real sense control what he says and how he says it in order for him to write effectively.[7] Giving students practice in writing about the same topic but assuming different speaking voices appears to be one of the most promising practices to come along in recent years. Teachers who have done so report that the activity gives many students a sense of control over their writing never before experienced.

Providing the time for the prewriting activities demanded by the new rhetoric is a problem in many schools, but promising curricular trends are appearing. An increasing number of schools are making provision for writing workshops and laboratories during the school day, sometimes as an elective course. Other schools have eliminated study halls, thus lengthening class periods and giving teachers additional time to help students with in-class writing and reading assignments. Even without this extra time, however, many teachers accomplish the same things through conferences, preliminary drafts, and buzz sessions with the students. In many classes, much more time is spent preparing for writing than in correcting what is written. As a matter of fact, available evidence suggests that a student will make fewer errors if he prepares for writing.

[6]Wayne Booth, "The Rhetorical Stance," *College Composition and Communication,* XIV (October, 1963), 139-45.

[7]Walker Gibson, "The Voice of the Writer," *College Composition and Communication,* XIII (October, 1962), 10-13.

EVALUATING STUDENT COMPOSITIONS

The whole matter of evaluation is beginning to take on a different function today. Although many teachers still insist on red-penciling every mechanical error a student makes as an indication of the degree of "correctness" he has achieved, many more are beginning to put their red pencils down in order to react more to what the student says in terms of *how* he says it — in other words, in terms of process. Lapses in spelling, punctuation, grammar, and syntax tend to be noted only when they interfere with the writer's intention and the reader's comprehension. Many teachers, recognizing that too many corrections can overwhelm a student and kill his enthusiasm, tend to concentrate on marking only one or two kinds of errors in a particular paper. Supposedly this practice allows a student to focus his attention more specifically on what he needs to improve.

Since reading and reacting to compositions are time-consuming tasks whatever the major emphasis in evaluation, several innovations are appearing which are aimed at easing the English teacher's paper load. The use of lay readers is a development which even in the face of much opposition appears to be increasing. The lay reader, usually a retired English teacher or qualified lay person, is often assigned to work with a specific teacher, and his duties vary depending upon the teacher. Sometimes he reads all of the compositions and corrects mechanical errors; sometimes he reads only three-fourths of the papers from a class and gives a complete evaluation while the regular teacher evaluates the others; and sometimes he evaluates only the first drafts. Although several studies have demonstrated the effectiveness of lay readers, most teachers still prefer to have a lighter teaching load and evaluate papers themselves.

The use of conferences during the school day as an evaluation procedure is increasing in popularity. Several new curriculum designs which provide for large-group, small-group, and individual instruction are appearing. Because it is flexible, team teaching gives teachers more opportunity to meet with individuals. Experimental programs, like one at Evanston Township High School, give teachers two days a week to have individual conferences. At Evanston, too, where secretarial help is available, teachers are experimenting with the use of dictaphones for recording their reactions to student themes. A secretary then types duplicate copies of the teacher's remarks, one for the student and one for the teacher. Some teachers report, however, that it takes as long to dictate remarks as to write them.

Not only as a time-saving device but as a practice which improves writing ability, student correction of themes is a prominent practice today. Working individually or in groups, students discuss their own or their peers' papers and evaluate them against a set of criteria developed with the help of the teacher. Teachers report that a student's peers tend to be more critical than the teacher, but they also report that careful analysis of another's writing frequently gives a student insight into his own. Commercial writing programs appearing now often give students directions for evaluating their own compositions.

With the current emphasis on process, rhetoric teachers are tending to de-emphasize the final product of a specific writing assignment. They are more apt today to evaluate a student's paper in terms of manifest growth in the command of process than in terms of its value as a final composition. With that aim, teachers are keeping cumulative folders of a student's written work as a way of gauging growth in the process of writing. Cumulative folders are also used to help provide continuity from year to year and from teacher to teacher. Examination of a student's folder allows a teacher to see what topics were treated previously, how they were handled, and what writing strengths and weaknesses are evident. Not an unimportant contribution, cumulative folders tend to eliminate overuse of the perennial stock writing assignments about favorite hobbies, places, and people. What teacher, seeing three writing assignments in the same folder on "The Most Interesting Thing I Did Last Summer," could make the same assignment again?

Another widespread method of measuring growth is the use of cumulative grids. The usual format for these grids is a listing down the left side of the paper of those items which the teacher considers when marking a paper and a series of columns across the paper, each representing a separate writing assignment. With each assignment, the teacher indicates on the grid the strengths and weaknesses of the paper. Items most commonly considered are content, organization, style, mechanics, and control of process. Grids vary in the number of items to be considered. Some list only gross features; others list minute characteristics.

Regardless of the criteria listed, however, grids have the advantage of letting the student know what the teacher considers important. They also force the teacher to consider elements of composition separately. Research indicates that grids tend to increase the correlation between one teacher's evaluation of a paper and another's. Research indicates, also, that good writers tend to vary more in the quality of successive writing assignments than do poor writers, a fact which indicates that the use of cumulative grids should enable teachers to evaluate potential and growth more accurately than they could if they relied on a single piece of writing as evidence.

However themes are evaluated, students are usually expected, and often required, to revise their papers and to practice those skills in which their writing demonstrates a weakness. The usual practice is to refer students to their composition texts or language handbooks for help in correcting errors, but with the increasing availability of programmed materials, there is a growing tendency to direct students to appropriate programs for developmental and remedial exercises. Some teachers demand repeated revision of a theme until it is a polished piece of writing, something the student can be proud of, but most teachers require only one revision.

LITERATURE IN THE RHETORIC PROGRAM

The study of literature has become an integral part of the study of rhetoric today. Formerly, literature study was used mainly as a source of topics. Teachers recognized that students had to write about something and believed that topics growing out of literature were more interesting and appropriate, especially for senior high school students, than those dealing with favorite people, hobbies, and personal events. The actual study of literature and composition was seldom correlated, however. Literature was studied and discussed, and compositions growing out of the discussions were assigned. The only correlation occurred in the choice of topics.

Today, however, one of the growing trends in teaching rhetoric is the use of good literature as a model for student writing. As a student gains insight into the structure of literature, he also gains insight into the writer's craft. Following this assumption, teachers are presenting more narrative and expository writing for possible imitation. Students analyze the writer's treatment of form, content, use of language and then try to apply what they have learned to their own writing. The emphasis is not so much on style as on craftsmanship, although some teachers do ask for duplication of style. For the most part, though, teachers want their students to note how the writer controls the many variables he must work with in order to achieve the desired effect. Writing assignments following such analysis require that the student produce a similar form, following the characteristics of the model they have studied. Such assignments, it is argued, give students a wider range of alternatives for expressing themselves and result in significantly better writing.

The use of literary modes also justifies the emphasis on process and structure of discourse in the new rhetoric. That emphasis, however, makes articulation of the composition program very difficult, for, as Bruner pointed out, process is not easily segmented. But the desire to sequence all phases of English instruction is very strong today. Some English educators have suggested articulating in terms of the length of writing assignments. They suggest increasing the length at each grade level, beginning with a few sentences of a paragraph in the seventh grade and ending with the longest papers in the twelfth. A student would begin with the writing of letters, proceed to short narrative papers, and then go on to fairly long expository pieces.

Consensus regarding articulation has certainly not been reached. The basic processes of composition still haven't been agreed upon. Teachers and writers, in spite of their attempts to discover just what it is that holds the key to success in writing, are still guessing. Surely the ability to manipulate symbols in order to communicate via the printed page is at the heart of the matter, but there is something else, too, if past success in teaching students to write effectively is an indication. As the search for that other ingredient continues, the teaching of written composition can be expected to change considerably in the next few years.

SELECTED REFERENCES

Booth, Wayne C. "The Revival of Rhetoric," *Publications of the Modern Language Association,* LXXX (May, 1965), 8-12.

Braddock, Richard, Richard Lloyd-Jones, and Lowell Schoer. *Research in Written Composition*. Champaign, Illinois: National Council of Teachers of English, 1963.

Brooks, Cleanth, and Robert Penn Warren. *Modern Rhetoric*. New York: Harcourt, Brace and World, Inc., 1958.

Burke, Virginia M. *The Lay Reader Program: Backgrounds and Procedures*. Wisconsin: Wisconsin Council of Teachers of English, 1961.

Burton, Dwight, and John Simmons. *Teaching English in Today's High Schools*. New York: Holt, Rinehart and Winston, Inc., 1964.

Corbin, Richard. *The Teaching of Writing in Our Schools*. New York: The Macmillan Company, 1966.

Gordon, Edward J., ed. *Writing and Literature in the Secondary School*. New York: Holt, Rinehart and Winston, Inc., 1965.

Judine, Sister M., IHM, ed. *A Guide for Evaluating Student Composition*. Champaign, Illinois: The National Council of Teachers of English, 1965.

Kitzhaber, Albert. *Themes, Theories, and Therapy: The Teaching of Writing in College*. New York: McGraw-Hill Book Company, 1959.

Martin, Harold, and Richard Ohmann. *The Logic and Rhetoric of Exposition*. Revised Edition. New York: Holt, Rinehart and Winston, Inc., 1963.

Roberts, Edgar. *Writing Themes About Literature*. Englewood Cliffs, New Jersey: Prentice-Hall, Inc., 1964.

Sherwood, John. *Discourse of Reason*. Second Edition. New York: Harper & Row, Publishers, 1964.

Smith, Eugene H. *Rhetoric and School Programs*. Champaign, Illinois: National Council of Teachers of English, 1966.

Strunk, William, Jr., and E. B. White. *The Elements of Style*. Revised Edition. New York: The Macmillan Company, 1959.

Toward a New Rhetoric. Reprint of October, 1963, issue of *College Composition and Communication*. Champaign, Illinois: National Council of Teachers of English, 1963.

Wilson, Grace, ed. *Composition Situations*. Champaign, Illinois: National Council of Teachers of English, 1966.

V

Language
and the New Method

Describing the characteristics of a language-centered curriculum, Priscilla Tyler wrote:

> What does it mean for the English course to be primarily the study of language? It does not mean merely the substitution of a new kind of grammar for an old kind of grammar. Rather, it implies broadening the philosophical context of teaching English.[1]

Even though the English curriculum is still not language-centered, the broadening of the philosophical context relating to the study of language which Tyler implied has begun to make its way into the English classroom. The study of language is becoming more personal, inductive, and descriptive; and it is focusing more on language as a tool which man can manipulate and change to suit his needs at a particular time in a particular context than as a static system of rules he must abide by at all times. The more accurate description of language which scholars in all areas of linguistic study have provided has led teachers to a different conception of what language is and how it operates. Out of that knowledge have come at least a few new guidelines for teaching.

For many years the study of language in high school was primarily the study of grammar, Latin grammar applied to English. When modern linguists challenged the accuracy of that grammar and the prescriptive teaching of grammar, they were

---

[1]Priscilla Tyler, "New Concepts and Content for the English Curriculum," *The English Leaflet,* LXI (Winter, 1962), 5.

attacking the sacred cow of the curriculum, the noblest of all studies. Teachers would not give it up easily. The new grammars — structural and transformational-generative — met with much resistance.

RESISTANCE TO NEW GRAMMARS

Many teachers were openly hostile to the new grammars, insisting that traditional grammar was perfectly adequate and that the new grammars merely supplied new labels for old containers. More than that, they could find no evidence that the new grammars were any more effective than the old in improving the skills of speaking and writing. To some, the new grammars with their emphasis on description rather than prescription represented a definite lowering of standards indicative of the country's moral decay.

In truth, much of the resistance to the new grammars was the result of ignorance. Teachers simply did not understand what the linguists were saying — as much a fault of the linguists as the teachers. Meeting after meeting found linguists presenting and discussing their theories in what seemed like an unknown tongue with no real attempt to communicate with the teachers in the audience. Linguistics appeared to be a study fit only for ivory towers; few teachers, even those who had spent time in those same towers, had taken any courses which would enlighten them. What most English teachers knew about grammar, they learned in high school from teachers and texts steeped in traditional grammar.

CURRENT STATE OF GRAMMAR

Today, much of the hostility has disappeared, and teachers are studying the new grammars, particularly transformational grammar. Teacher education institutions are beginning to require more courses in all phases of language study, particularly history of language, rhetoric, and grammar. School systems are sponsoring in-service workshops for English teachers so that they can study linguistics and develop materials, and the federal government is financing institutes for the same purpose. Linguists are beginning to write more readable texts. And some educators, notably Paul Roberts and Neil Postman, have written language texts based on the new grammars for junior and senior high school use. Nevertheless, an occasional impassioned defense of traditional grammar can still be heard along with many more calls, in the name of reason, for the adoption of an eclectic grammar.

Even if a new classroom grammar should crystallize out of the current state of flux, the study of grammar, as such, will hopefully never receive as much emphasis in the curriculum as before. The statement that every youngster has the grammar of his language built into him by the time he reaches school age has been repeated so often that teachers have come to believe it and to question the value of teaching what the student already knows. Those who are currently advocating the study of grammar as an end in itself or as a mental discipline are not apt to have as wide an audience in today's utilitarian world.

Clearly, the new grammars will make a greater impact on the English curriculum if it can be demonstrated that knowledge of them improves writing ability. H. A. Gleason, Jr., in one of the newest linguistic texts,[2] asserts that if the composing process can be taught, a study of grammar with the following aims should be useful:

> First, the teacher should aim at increasing sensitivity to structure and to alternatives in structure, that is, to the subject matter of grammar. For free and fluent writing, this means strengthened competence in the student's internalized grammar of literary English, and the assimilation of additional structural patterns.[3]

The new grammars with their emphasis on syntactic structures may be suited to the task which Gleason has identified for the teacher; there is evidence already appearing in the work of Hunt[4] and Christensen[5] that ability to manipulate syntactic structures is related to writing ability. But as indicated in the chapter on

    [2]H. A. Gleason, Jr., *Linguistics and English Grammar* (New York: Holt, Rinehart and Winston, Inc., 1965).
    [3]*Ibid.,* p. 476.
    [4]Kellogg W. Hunt, "A Synopsis of Clause-to-Sentence Length Factors," *The English Journal,* LIV (April, 1965), 300-309.
    [5]Francis Christensen, "A Generative Rhetoric of the Sentence," *College Composition and Communication,* XIV (October, 1963), 155-61.

composition, knowledge of semantics, usage, and thought processes are also related to writing ability; and in today's high school English curriculum, as well as tomorrow's, the study of grammar seems destined to play a subordinate role to a more general study of language as a system of communication which has as one characteristic a pattern of regular syntactic relationships which the native speaker automatically follows.

CONTEXTUAL STUDY OF GRAMMAR

When students do study grammar today, they often study it in the context of their own language with an emphasis on discovering what recurrent patterns they habitually use and what alternative patterns are available to use. Teachers have long doubted the transfer value of grammar exercises using sentences bearing little or no resemblance to those the students would use, and there is certainly a trend away from that practice.

There is also a trend away from stopping grammatical analysis once the pattern in question has been identified. Since ability to apply knowledge is the test of learning, students are being required to go beyond identification to application, which in the case of grammar knowledge, means to the creation of new sentences. This emphasis on the study of grammar as a means of generating a variety of sentences has led to a de-emphasis on tearing sentences apart. Even the new language texts and programed language materials are designed so that the student who uses them is building sentences, not taking them apart. The study of grammar today, then, focuses as much on variety and effectiveness of style as on correctness of expression and encourages students to seek the most effective construction for carrying the intended lexical content.

USAGE AND APPROPRIATENESS

Because students are more apt to make errors involving usage than grammar, usage and the doctrine of appropriateness are replacing grammar and the doctrine of correctness. At one time grammar and usage were considered nearly synonymous, but today they have come to represent entirely different aspects of language study. Grammar represents the system of language, the regularity which is built into it. Usage, on the other hand, represents the alternatives available within the system. Related to the study of usage is the study of dialect, which usually refers to the characteristic usage patterns of a group or an individual. Characteristic choices of words, pronunciation, and structures usually distinguish one dialect from another. Usage, because it offers the individual a choice, is more consciously controlled than grammar, and teachers are teaching control based on appropriateness.

The emphasis on appropriate usage is especially strong in schools having a culturally disadvantaged population. The culturally disadvantaged are usually members of some subcultural group, and often the dialect of their group is the only one they are familiar with. Characterized by a very limited background with few, if any, contacts outside of their immediate surroundings and little or no contact with books in the home, the culturally disadvantaged often lack linguistic versatility. Their conversation is usually limited to their own peer group. Of course, they have contacts with teachers who speak a different dialect, but for the most part the teacher's dialect is inappropriate for the cultural context in which the students live.

Because culturally disadvantaged students want desperately to master the standard American dialect as a means of escaping from the confines of their narrow social and economic environment, they attach great value to "correct" usage. They know how important "good" usage is as a measure of education and "culture." Negro leaders today, for instance, show little regard for the psycholinguist's concern over possible personality damage which can result from a student's rejection of the language of his home; they are more concerned over the personality damage which can result from being limited by the language of his home to a menial, low-paying job. Facility with language is viewed as a means to upward mobility.

The problems involved in teaching the standard American dialect to students from culturally disadvantaged homes are just beginning to be attacked in a major way, but the insights into language and its development which linguists have supplied are providing the basis for experimentation. Linguists have reasserted the primacy of oral language, and therefore, most of the new language programs for the disadvantaged begin with extensive and intensive oral practice. Students are given an opportunity to communicate in a variety of oral situations: discussions, conversations, speeches, and interviews. Such practice helps to develop a sense of appropriate language for the situation. Much of the practice work is recorded on tape so that students can hear and analyze their use of language. Language laboratories are being used to give them practice hearing and reproducing different dialects. Following oral work, or along with it, is practice in writing and reading. As with beginning readers and writers, the progression here is from the sound to its graphic representation.

LANGUAGE AND READING

The teaching of reading skills is demanding increasingly more attention on the high school level, particularly, again, with the culturally disadvantaged. Lacking experiences with books and the language usage encountered in them, a great many culturally disadvantaged students immediately fall behind students at their age and grade level, and their reading deficiency tends to continue with them throughout school and to affect their performance in all academic areas. As a matter of fact, inability to read well appears to be one of the factors related to school drop-out. Although the reading problem is most severe in large urban areas, it has grown to such proportions throughout the country that many states now specify that English teachers must have a course in teaching reading in order to qualify for certification. Social promotion, poor teaching in elementary school, home background, and the changing role of reading in our culture are only a few of the factors usually blamed for the reading problem, but whatever the cause, it is a language problem which seems to be growing in proportions.

The reading problem is being attacked in a number of ways. Some schools, especially junior high schools, provide for reading improvement classes in addition to regular English classes, while others have set up reading laboratories which students must attend on a regular basis. In most schools, though, the problem is left to the regular classroom teacher to deal with in the context of his subject. Teachers who initially scoffed at the slogan that every teacher should be a teacher of reading have discovered that, indeed, much of their time must be spent teaching students the vocabulary and syntax peculiar to the printed materials in their subject field.

A great bulk of materials designed specifically for teaching reading skills in secondary schools is beginning to appear, much of it based on the contributions made by structural linguists in the accurate description of the oral and written signaling systems in English and the differences between them. One of the characteristics of the new materials is their greater attention to the characteristics of language than to the characteristics of the reading act. There was a time when most reading materials seemed to concentrate on such reading habits as developing proper eye movements and increasing eye span as activities operating independently of the reading material, but today the new reading materials reflect the notion that the key to successful reading is the ability to translate the printed word into speech.

Teaching reading requires two kinds of materials: one for improving skills and another for using them. A reading program will occasionally fail simply because it didn't provide for both. If a student does nothing but exercises in skill improvement, he soon loses interest because he doesn't have an opportunity to test his improvement with other materials. On the other hand, if a student does nothing but read materials geared to his present level of reading ability, he is doing nothing to improve it. Fortunately, both kinds of materials are available.

A teacher can obtain many high-interest, low-ability materials for use in improving reading skills. Often they are packaged and arranged in a sequence of increasing difficulty for the student to follow. And particularly within the last ten years, the amount of high-interest, low-reading-level materials, usually short stories and junior novels, available for practice and leisure reading has greatly expanded. The well-written junior novel, because it allows a student to read a story of interest to him on a level he can comprehend, must be considered one of the most effective tools the teacher has at his command for keeping some students interested in reading and in developing literary appreciation.

THE STUDY OF SEMANTICS

Crucial to the study of reading, as to all other language activities, is the study of semantics. In any language-centered curriculum or any curriculum which stresses communication, both of which are becoming more common, semantics must be a central concern. Entire courses of study based on semantic concepts with literature and composition as areas of investigation and experimentation are being currently developed and tested. Such a course of study has been developed by James McCrimmon at the University of Illinois High School, and it has been tested with great success in junior and senior high schools throughout Illinois.

The McCrimmon materials, and others like them, lean heavily on the work of Korzybski, I. A. Richards, Hayakawa, and Walpole for their major concepts. The basic concept, of course, is that language is an arbitrary set of symbols which, by agreement of the people who use them, convey meaning. Another is that the meaning which is communicated is affected by the experiences of the sender and receiver, their relationship to each other, and the context in which the communication takes place. Connotation and denotation are also stressed, as is metaphor. Abstraction and levels of abstractions are included, too, as important concepts. Heavy emphasis is given to the student's knowing report from inference and being able to distinguish statements of desire from statements of fact, statements of opinion from statements of fact, and statements of objective description from statements of personal response. A basic concept a student should understand is the relationship between the word and the thing it represents.

These semantic concepts have, of course, been taught outside the context of a language-centered curriculum, but like many other language concepts, they seldom have been taught in a systematic way. Most often they have been taught in relation to particular points in a particular piece of literature or a particular writing assignment, stopping short of the level of generalization. What is being done now, however, is to teach semantics as an organized body of knowledge that pertains to all aspects of communication.

THE TEACHING LAG

Old practices do not easily give way to new ones. The teaching of language in some schools still consists of grammar on Mondays and Tuesdays and spelling on Fridays. Spelling and vocabulary lists featuring words like "blitzkrieg" and "aeroplane" still constitute the entire spelling and vocabulary programs in some schools. A noun is still the name of a person, place, or thing; and a pronoun still takes the place of a noun in some classrooms. Diagramming is still the test of language mastery as far as many teachers are concerned. The use of "ain't" is still considered a grammatical error, as is the ending of a sentence with a preposition. And workbook exercises with sentence like "Mother, (can, may) I fix the tea? asked Tim." still serve as the basic practice materials in some programs. All of those practices are still with us even though they are gradually disappearing.

Obviously, those practices disappeared from many schools long ago, but unfortunately, when they went so did all study of language as a separate area of investigation. Language, as such, is simply not being taught in many schools. The void created by the absence of traditional grammar instruction was never filled. Many teachers have been waiting for the dust to settle over the grammar battlefield before committing themselves to any of the combatants. Sensing a change in the making, they have waited.

The direction and dimensions of change have finally begun to emerge, and they have little to do with grammar. The broadening of the philosophical context of English teaching advocated by Tyler appears to be coming about, and the study of language appears to be gaining favor as the center of the English curriculum. Literature and composition are apt to be studied in the future as functions of language and to be analyzed from the standpoint of determining how language functions as a means of communication and a mirror of man's past and present. The study of grammar is apt to receive less attention than usage and semantics. Language study is apt to become more inductive and descriptive, with emphasis on discovering what constitutes language, how it works, how it changes, and how it relates to the individual as he attempts to find and express meaning in his world.[6]

SELECTED REFERENCES

Allen, Harold B., ed. *Readings in Applied English Linguistics.* New York: Appleton-Century-Crofts, 1964.

Allen, Harold B., and Others. *New Dimensions in English.* Wichita: McCormick-Mathers Publishing Company, Inc., 1966.

Anderson, Wallace L., and Norman C. Stageberg, eds. *Introductory Readings on Language.* New York: Holt, Rinehart and Winston, Inc., 1962.

Barbe, Walter, ed. *Teaching Reading: Selected Materials.* New York: Oxford University Press, 1965.

Bateman, Donald, and Frank Zedonis. *The Effect of a Study of Transformational Grammar on the Writing of Ninth and Tenth Graders.* Champaign, Illinois: National Council of Teachers of English, 1966.

Burton, Dwight, and John Simmons. *Teaching English in Today's High Schools.* New York: Holt, Rinehart and Winston, Inc., 1965.

Corbin, Richard, and Muriel Crosby, eds. *Language Programs for the Disadvantaged.* The Report of the NCTE Task Force on Teaching English to the Disadvantaged. Champaign, Illinois: The National Council of Teachers of English, 1965.

Dechant, Emerald. *Improving the Teaching of Reading.* Englewood Cliffs, New Jersey: Prentice-Hall, Inc., 1964.

Emig, Janet A., James T. Fleming, and Helen M. Popp, eds.

[6]Hopefully, this trend will not be impeded by secondary teachers who are so intrigued by generative-transformational grammar that they might allow it to take over their language program.

Language and Learning. New York: Harcourt, Brace & World, Inc., 1966.

Fries, Charles C. *Linguistics and Reading.* New York: Holt, Rinehart and Winston, Inc., 1962.

Gleason, H. A., Jr. *Linguistics and English Grammar.* New York: Holt, Rinehart and Winston, Inc., 1965.

Goldstein, Miriam B. *The Teaching of Language in Our Schools.* New York: The Macmillan Company, 1966.

Guth, Hans P. *English Today and Tomorrow.* Englewood Cliffs, New Jersey: Prentice-Hall, Inc., 1964.

Hayakawa, S. I. *Language in Thought and Action.* New York: Harcourt, Brace & World, Inc., 1964.

Hazard, Patrick D., and Mary E. Hazard, eds. *Language and Literacy Today.* Chicago: Science Research Associates, 1965.

Hogan, Robert F., ed. *The English Language in the School Program.* Champaign, Illinois: National Council of Teachers of English, 1966.

Loban, Walter. *Problems in Oral English.* Champaign, Illinois: National Council of Teachers of English, 1966.

Malmstrom, Jean, and Annabel Ashley. *Dialects, U.S.A.* Champaign, Illinois: National Council of Teachers of English, 1963.

McDavid, Ravin. *American Social Dialects.* Champaign, Illinois: National Council of Teachers of English, 1965.

———. ed. *An Examination of the Attitudes of the NCTE Toward Language.* Research Report No. 4. Champaign, Illinois: National Council of Teachers of English, 1965.

Moulton, William G. *Linguistics and Language Teaching in the United States 1940-1960.* Washington, D.C.: U. S. Government Printing Office, 1963.

National Council of Teachers of English. *The Sentence and the Paragraph.* Champaign, Illinois: National Council of Teachers of English, 1966.

Nist, John. *A Structural History of English.* New York: St. Martin's Press, 1966.

Pooley, Robert C. *Teaching English Grammar.* New York: Appleton-Century-Crofts, Inc., 1957.

Reeves, Ruth. *The Teaching of Reading in Our Schools.* New York: The Macmillan Company, 1966.

Rogovin, Syrell. *Modern English Sentence Structure.* New York: Random House, Inc., 1964.

Stageberg, Norman. *An Introductory English Grammar.* New York: Holt, Rinehart and Winston, Inc., 1965.

Thomas, Owen. *Transformational Grammar and the Teacher of English.* New York: Holt, Rinehart and Winston, Inc., 1965.

Tyler, Priscilla, ed. *Linguistics and Reading: A Second Symposium.* Champaign, Illinois: National Council of Teachers of English, 1966.

Walters, Theodore W. *The Georgetown Bibliography of Studies Contributing to the Psycholinguistics of Language Learning.* Washington, D.C.: Georgetown University Press, 1966.

VI

Ways of
Assessing Change

Today English educators assume that teachers and researchers who are experimenting with new developments are attempting to impart new knowledge about the subject and new insights into the structure of the subject, and that such things can be taught in ways that will develop in students effective methods of inquiry in the subject. English educators also assume that methods of inquiry can lead students to *independent* generalizations about the nature and use of English.

Are students acquiring these new competencies? What behavioral changes stand as some proof of these competencies? In what ways are these competencies and the resulting behavioral changes beneficial to students today? In what ways might today's education in English prepare each student for tomorrow's society?

English teachers cannot know the answer to even the first question raised above unless they find new and improved ways of assessing change. Little progress will be made unless two gaps are closed quickly: (1) the gap between theories, methods, and tools in the teaching of English on one hand and tests and measurements on the other, and (2) the gap between technical developments in tests and measurements and the test-user or English teacher. The traditional image of the English teacher as the professionally secretive and isolated author of essay questions, pop quizzes, and true-false questions is vanishing. Closer attention to new developments in the teaching of English and to the learning process of individual students is involving more teachers in the selection of standardized tests, in the cooperative development of improved teacher-made tests, and in the analysis and use of information from both standardized tests and teacher-made tests. Attention to tests and measurements has been delayed too long in English, but it is now gathering enough strength to be called a trend. This development, which must stay even with all others if progress is to be made, cannot possibly make its contribution without the full support of practicing English teachers. For this reason, this chapter will regard the English teacher as the central figure in finding and using new ways of assessing change.

ASSESSMENTS IN LITERATURE

TESTING FOR LEVELS OF THINKING

By supporting inductive teaching and close textual analysis, more teachers are asking students to study literature inductively. In class discussions, teachers who ask *what, what next, when, where,* and *how* or *in what way* more often ask *why.* As students study and discuss a piece of literature which has conceptual levels far beyond its readability level, alert teachers are taking many opportunities to involve slower students by soliciting from them answers which lay the foundation for questions that challenge the best minds in the class. In directing group reading and in providing wide, individualized reading (often immediately following the study of a literary type in common), teachers are giving students opportunities to discover that generalizations should be enlarged, drawn into sharper focus, or altered. And, as teachers teach inductively, they appear to be more conscious of the five "levels of teaching and testing" outlined by Gordon: "(1) to remember a fact, (2) to prove a generalization that some-one else has made, (3) to make one's own generalization, (4) to generalize from the book to its application to life, and finally, (5) to carry over the generalization into one's own behavior."[1]

Preoccupation with two kinds of questions, however, still

[1] Edward J. Gordon, "Levels of Teaching and Testing," *The English Journal,* XLIV (September, 1955), 331. Reprinted by permission of the National Council of Teachers of English.

prevents many teachers and students from moving above the second level described above. The first kind is the *what-happens-next* question, which takes most of the promise and life out of class discussion. The second kind appears often as an "essay" question. This is the *what-do-you-think-about-what-has-been-said* question, the one that states a generalization which has been reached by someone else and asks the student to comment after the fact. The first question asks for details in sequence (useful only in testing a student's ability to remember the chronology of events), and the second checks up to see whether a main idea is residual. Neither requires much thinking.

Surely questions can lead to higher levels of thought. Surely they can stimulate a fresh point of view, even inquiry into the structural relationships of literary works not studied in class. Suppose a literary selection gives students an excellent opportunity to pick up clues to the nature of characters in many of the same ways that students learn about people in life. By asking students not just to describe a character but to tell how they have learned certain things about the character, the teacher is asking them to consider whether the author has used any of the following methods of revealing and developing a character:

1. Telling what kind of person he is
2. Describing the person, his clothing, and his environment
3. Showing his actions
4. Letting him talk
5. Relating his thoughts
6. Showing how other people talk to him
7. Showing what other people say about him
8. Showing how other people react because of him
9. Showing how he reacts to others[2]

By asking students to think of three or four words which describe a character most effectively at the beginning and at the end of a story or novel, and to defend their choice by referring to examples in the work, the teacher is inviting them to review everything that has caused the character to change and to draw these influences into sharp focus. A teacher should ask questions which invite considerations of cause and effect—things just do not happen—probability, plausibility, and the various inter-

[2]J. N. Hook, *The Teaching of High School English,* pp. 174-75. Third Edition, Copyright © 1965 The Ronald Press Company, New York.

relationships among characters, plot, setting, theme, and style. If carefully worked into the phrasing of questions, generalizations reached by students in class can point the way not only toward the total view of life pictured by the total structure of a work, but even to a personal consideration of how this view could make a difference in their own lives. Thus, a student can be urged to think on the highest level mentioned by Gordon.

Teachers can also experiment with various ways to guide, test, and retest a student's thinking as he is carried to higher levels of thought by test questions. Questions that begin with such particulars as *what* and *when* could build progressively and cumulatively by steps, as in programed "frames," to more sophisticated questions. Such a test might concern a work which students have not studied. At various points along the way, students might be asked to compare, contrast, synthesize, reconsider, and comment critically in short pieces of writing. In brief, there might be some value in programing test items which would occasionally ask students to "branch" into an explanation or verification of some point in the development of their answers. By doing so, teachers might move a little closer to making tests which are teaching tools as well.

Objective tests in literature might stimulate more thinking than they have in the past. For example, the versatile multiple-choice item type can contain choices — not "distractors" — on several levels of sophistication. Such choices might be weighted according to the level of critical thinking, abstraction, or maturity they demand. The score on such a test would not represent a total of "right" answers, minus a penalty for guessing, but a level of thinking. For example, a teacher might use a question such as this one, after students have read *The Pearl,* a novel by Steinbeck.

In the opening lines of the novel, Steinbeck describes "a morning like other mornings and yet perfect among mornings." However, in the midst of this description, a small dusty ant struggles frantically to escape the sand trap an ant lion has dug. Which statement below is in your opinion the best explanation of why the struggle of an ant for his life appears in the peaceful setting of a "perfect" morning?
A. It adds interest to the story; the rest of the description would seem dull without it.
B. It indicates that even the smallest things and events will be described in this novel.

C. It suggests that such struggle is a part of the system of things, or just the way life is.
D. It suggests that Kino or someone in his family will soon be attacked.
E. It gives the reader a little shock, so that the scorpion's sting will not come as too great a shock.[3]

These choices range from the relatively unsophisticated observations in A, B, and E to the possibility of foreshadowing in D, and to the sophisticated consideration in C of a non-teleological attitude, an acceptance of life as it is. Prompted by the idea in choice C, some students may wish to discuss the implications of Kino's attempt to be the teleologist, a character who will not accept his "deep participation with all things," or life itself, for what it is.

REACHING THE INDIVIDUAL STUDENT

Nothing has given so much impetus to wide individual reading as the "paperback revolution." Found in prepared teaching units sold as packaged classroom libraries, ordered by teachers and students from distributors, kept in English bookrooms for supplementary use, and found in thousands of paperback bookstores in high schools, the paperback has placed "little" books in the hands of many students who might shy away from the same titles in hard cover. Using reading "designs" and "ladders," teachers have attempted to provide steps to greater maturity in reading literature.

In recognition of this increased and varied use of books, some publishing companies have taken the novel out of the anthology, have substituted discussion guides on several novels, and have even offered their own inexpensive paperback editions replete with discussion guides, critical commentary, background information, and study questions.

Paperback "units" have given teachers effective ways of providing an intensive and extensive study of literature which is highly individualized. Bantam Books, Inc., has designed "Learning Units," which consist of packaged classroom libraries of selected paperbacks. The books vary in difficulty and, with the aid of lesson plans, provide a study of a genre or literary type,

[3]From "A Short-Answer Test on *The Pearl*," by William H. Evans.

such as the novel or play, or a consideration of several points of view on a topic or theme. "Scholastic Literature Units" (Scholastic Magazines and Book Services), which are generally thematic in organization, have very successfully provided an organized way of breaking lockstep teaching in literature. In such prepared classroom units, the selection of books and the choice of questions vary in difficulty and maturity. In the hands of competent English teachers, who are of course the best judges of how to adapt and enrich a paperback unit in the best interests of individual students, such materials can provide an excellent way of moving students a step at a time toward greater understanding and appreciation of literature. In this effort, however, the teacher must construct any additional questions and study guides which seem to provide promising steps and catalysts in class discussion, group discussion, and independent reading and study. Since some phases of such units provide for individualized self-instruction, the teacher is free for very profitable one-to-one conferences with students about their reading.

Amid the current deluge of books, it is easy to imagine that some teachers feel too overwhelmed to ask questions dealing with such specifics as identifying characters and quotations or describing the significance of an incident or a symbol. But all questions do not have to be specific to provide for individual differences while urging students to higher levels of thinking. For example, the following questions by Professor Gordon invite reactions from individuals of varying abilities and seek the highest level in teaching and testing: "Take any novel that you have read this year and show how it has aided your understanding of another person," or "In some story that you have read, point out the most important decision of the main character; then show how the author prepared you for that decision."[4]

Questions such as those just mentioned can also provide opportunities for students to go to their books for examples which support or question generalizations being reached by the class, no matter how literature study is organized. A focus on point of view might prompt many interesting examples of point of view in various books. Students might also illustrate how authors adjust style to suit the purpose and tone of a literary selection, describe a scene, and give unity to an idea or theme.

[4]Gordon, *op. cit.,* p. 334.

Whether teachers use annotated and edited editions, prepared paperback units, or teacher-made units based on books selected in cooperation with students, one fact should be stressed. Wall-to-wall paperbacks provide many promising opportunities for the individualized study of literature, but they do not by themselves constitute a good individualized reading program. Success may depend upon two factors: (1) a structured teaching situation, which really provides for individual differences and really tries to urge students by steps to greater maturity in reading literature; and (2) assessment directed at measuring changes in an individual's growth in understanding and taste, not at measuring only the progress of a class. In this last effort, teachers might consider experimenting with various kinds of attitude scales, interview techniques, case study techniques, and some of the latest techniques for observing student behavior and change. The *Handbook of Research on Teaching* (Rand McNally & Company, 1963) contains descriptions of procedures which could be adapted by the English teacher.

ASSESSING WRITING ABOUT LITERATURE

The current interest in using literature as a source for writing springs from several hopes. One teacher may feel that there is no better source for ideas which the student can relate to life. Another may believe that there is value in asking students to imitate the writing of professionals. Another may be convinced that controlled research with "casebooks" will eliminate plagiarism. Still another may feel that students need to know how to write about literature. In the last case, the teacher will give instruction on how to write summaries, critiques, and analyses. In recognition of this trend, anthologists have recently included brief lessons or "guidelines" for composition. Composition questions in anthologies now ask students to organize a piece of writing in a certain way in answering a question about a selection. Books devoted exclusively to teaching how to write about literature also stress this kind of control and direction.

Control and *direction* are, in fact, key words in characterizing the trend. The English teacher can expect to see an increasing number of questions that outline rather specifically the way in which students are expected to organize a piece of writing about literature. In constructing such questions and in using them, the real problem will be that of achieving balance between freedom and control. The sources may seem much more fertile, and the opportunities to *teach* students how to organize their writing may seem much more promising. But, will students be encouraged to think for themselves? Will they have enough freedom to develop power, rhythm, and style in writing? Models, guidelines, individualized laboratory practice, conferences, individual pretesting and retesting, and an articulated writing program should aid in solving this problem.

ASSESSMENTS IN WRITTEN COMPOSITION

Teaching Rhetoric in the Schools

Closely allied with the increasing attention to literature as a source for writing is the revival of classical principles of rhetoric. English educators are probably justified in doubting that much which has been called composition ever was composition. It is probably true that many teachers have been so busy making a blue and red collage of corrections in punctuation, capitalization, grammar, usage, and spelling on student papers, that they have not taught students how to place thoughts together persuasively on paper, and to arrange and combine elements to form a unified piece of writing. In any case, there does seem to be a stir of interest in classical principles of rhetoric as guidelines to writing. One high school text uses literature selections as "a key to writing," presents twenty-five lessons, each developing "a rhetorical skill or a composition skill approached through rhetoric," and declares that "there is no point in attempting less."[5]

It is difficult to say how strong the influence of classical rhetoric will be, but it seems safe to assume that teachers will place even greater stress on expository writing, and that they will give students more directions on how to analyze the rhetorical appeal, the function, and the devices in a model. Objective tests may ask for more judgments about rhetorical skills in a selection and in suggested revisions of that selection. The added attention to rhetorical skills in objective writing tests will

[5]Don P. Brown and Others, *Writing: Unit Lessons in Composition* (New York: Ginn and Company, 1964), p. iv.

probably reveal no more than a knowledge of such skills. The increased attention to specific guidelines or controls in actual writing assignments, on the other hand, might prove helpful in improving skills, especially if teachers limit their constructive remarks on student papers to the particular skills which they ask students to demonstrate.

ASSESSING A "NEW" RHETORIC

If a "new" rhetoric is emerging, no one seems prepared to guess what it will be. English educators hope that minds as inquiring as those which now investigate language and literature will discover new knowledge about writing, or even develop a descriptive or generative system for written discourse. Some linguists have, in fact, alluded to the grammar between sentences and to the syntax of the paragraph.

One piece of research might let in enough light to guide a breakthrough. In a very intensive study of writing in the fourth, eighth, and twelfth grades, Kellogg Hunt found the greatest evidence of maturity in writing to be the number of subordinate clauses or kernel sentences embedded within main clauses. Hunt suggests "sentence building" dealing with "sentence-combining transformations," and also urges the teacher to find out much more about "what happens inside those clauses that they become so decisively longer in the hands of older and better writers."[6] An interesting speculation is that further investigations of sentence-combining transformations which lead to longer "T-units" (minimal terminable units) can bring teachers into much closer agreement about "good" writing. Explored more fully, Hunt's "T-unit" of maturity – or future evidence related to it – could be extremely helpful in evaluating writing.

DESIGNING FOR EVALUATION

Amid demands for more writing, a multitude of designs have been invented to facilitate evaluation. Most of these have been discussed at some length in Chapter 4. Educated lay citizens have

[6]Kellogg W. Hunt, "A Synopsis of Clause-to-Sentence Length Factors," *The English Journal*, LIV (April, 1965), 309. Hunt's study was done as Cooperative Research Project No. 1998, U. S. Office of Education. The complete report is available from the National Council of Teachers of English under the title *Grammatical Structures Written at Three Grade Levels*.

been paid to grade papers for English teachers. Students, using criteria which they have helped to develop, evaluate papers written by classmates. In some schools, class size has been reduced to twenty-five or less, and the total student load has been reduced to about one hundred. In other schools, teachers have established writing "laboratory" periods in order to narrow and individualize the focus on skills taught. More teachers have used individual profile charts or "grids" to record individual strengths and weaknesses, and these grids are kept with each student's papers in his personal cumulative writing file. Transparencies and other visual aids have been used to focus the attention of a class or a small group on a student's paper or on a professional piece of writing which serves as a model. Teachers who have been fortunate enough to have secretarial help have dictated their corrections and comments. These are typed and attached to a student's paper. Teachers without secretaries have asked students to use earphones to listen individually to recorded evaluations of their papers while other students work in a laboratory-type writing session.

As indicated in Chapter 4, some innovations may be greater aids to evaluating themes than others. For example, a reduced class load may provide better opportunities to really help individual students than a lay reader program. Use of the tape recorder may not be as effective as an individual conference. In assessing the value of an innovation which has been established in the face of overwhelming student loads, the teacher must ask whether the innovation helps students as much as other persons say it will. If students are helped in ways that would not be possible without the innovation, the new approach is indeed promising. If it is little more than a convenience for teachers or school administrators, it has not earned its keep.

NEW ASSESSMENTS IN LANGUAGE

In creating new tests in grammar, teachers will need to be clearer about what they are teaching and testing. If a test is designed to test knowledge of grammar, can the teacher claim to measure anything else? Certainly this is all that can be expected of traditional tests which test knowledge of traditional Latinized-English grammar. Because they test mainly the recognition of generalizations and labels, the ability to proofread someone's writing for predetermined errors, and the recognition and use of a system which attempts to diagram syntax as a visual aid, tests in traditional grammar ask for nothing more than identification. Many tests in structural linguistics expect little more than a check-up of knowledge about that system. Using such tests, can teachers claim any other purpose than to determine whether a student knows new terms, can assign new labels to certain predetermined linguistic patterns, and can construct an elaborate visual aid patterned after the one presented in a book?

Asking for generalizations about the positions and forms of nonsense words in various kinds of nonsense clusters and patterns, as structuralists often do, will not test more than recognition of form and structural function. Asking students to judge whether this or that sentence already fits a structural pattern or might be made to fit by adding, moving, or deleting words is asking for judgment after the fact. Giving students controlled ingredients in lists of words or in scrambled phrases and asking them to order these elements into acceptable patterns tests demonstration of a sort but not use.

An English teacher might come closer to testing use of the language by providing the following directions: "Write a sentence of your own, starting with the word *before*. Tell about something that you wanted to do. In the second part of the sentence, tell about a startling event that prevented you from doing what you wanted to do." Students might compare their sentences with acceptable model sentences; they might also compare similarities and differences among their own sentences.

Teaching and testing for knowledge should not be regarded as a compromise; the acquisition of knowledge is a very important part of one's competence in language. But if an English teacher's purpose *is* to test only a student's knowledge of how the English language is described, he has two very important obligations. First, he should test for this knowledge and not imply that a high score is any sure indication of greater skill in using language. Most of the research in the teaching and testing of grammar still supports this view. Secondly, he should incorporate in his tests, as in his teaching, new knowledge whenever it becomes apparent that this knowledge is more accurate.

Faced by a very rapid accumulation of new data about language, even by new systems and the possibility of more systems for describing the language, the English teacher must be especially careful that his teacher-made tests test what he expects his students to know. He has the right to expect standardized tests to stay fairly even with the most accurate knowledge available. But before drawing conclusions about local norms and individual achievement, he must take into account the similarities and the differences between what he teaches and tests and what standardized tests test.

TESTING THE METHOD OF INQUIRY

More English teachers are beginning to see the advantage of teaching from particulars to student-made generalizations. One promising method is to set up a situation problem which invites students to observe data, perceive common elements, state a generalization, test it through further analysis, and modify it. Tapes of spoken language provide evidence which students use in making spoken or written generalizations about such matters as levels of usage, dialect, or the usefulness of intonation in learning punctuation. If a teacher hopes to find out whether a student has command of a system of inquiry—a method of thinking in his subject—the teacher must test for the means as well as the end. After the class has solved a problem, a teacher could give a test which presents new data and a problem in language similar to the problem which just confronted the class. Excellent examples of this procedure can be seen in two books by Neil Postman: *Discovering Your Language* and *The Uses of Language* (Holt, Rinehart and Winston, Inc.).

ASSESSING ORAL PATTERN PRACTICE

Another interesting development in English is the increasing experimentation with oral "pattern practice." Procedures resemble those now used in teaching foreign languages and in teaching English as a second language. Limited evidence seems to indicate that an oral approach is effective in creating in students an awareness of usages in English which are different from their own. With the aid of tapes and printed oral activities, the English teacher leads students through listening and speaking practices which include conversations, substitution drills, and dialogues. Students hear and speak words appropriate at the standard level of usage. The procedure is not a stamping-out process, which might seem to imply that usage on lower levels is "wrong" or does not communicate effectively in a student's home or neighborhood.

Following such oral activities, how sensible is it to administer a paper-and-pencil recognition test? Should not tapes and oral readings take the place of printed tests, especially for poor readers? Under what circumstances might tapes and printed tests be used together to give students opportunities to look at standard usage as they hear it? Should tests ask certain students to work usage into exercises, scripts, and dialogues for their own oral activities, thus carrying the usage immediately into their own speaking and writing?

CONSIDERING THE LANGUAGE SPECTRUM

The expanding scope of language study — which is leading to semantics, etymology, usage, and dialectology in both the elementary and secondary schools — has prompted more teachers to ask students about intriguing interrelationships among the various aspects of language found in literature, persuasive speeches, and advertising copy. More teachers are asking students to look at language, to listen to language, to consider the power of words and the ways in which a writer puts his thinking together and adjusts his style to suit his purpose. Some questions are quite specific and ask whether a certain word, if substituted for another in the same context, would be as appropriate or as effective. Such approaches are currently used, even in standardized tests, but they will become more experimental in light of broad concerns about language, deep concerns about close reading, and the general concern about critical thinking. Semantics and vocabulary study will lead to a greater use of analogies, to problems in communication, attitude scales, perhaps even to semantic differential tests in semantics.

REACHING THE INDIVIDUAL

Increased attempts to offer individualized instruction in language must also be considered in constructing tests. Tapes and other "language laboratory" equipment, programed materials, flexible scheduling, and non-graded classes have provided small but significant starts in the secondary schools. But a teacher cannot really help his students individually unless he can diagnose and then test for gain on an individual basis. A teacher must discover knowledge and skills which students already have and *do not need,* he must discover individual needs, and he must test for and record individual growth.

Perhaps the workings of individualized instruction in language can be more clearly shown by describing briefly two ways of organizing instruction. Plan I provides for group instruction in a traditional way; Plan II provides for individualized instruction.

Plan I is based on the assumption that students who have not done well on departmental tests of minimum essentials in grammar and usage, on standardized tests largely of the proofreading variety, and in written work should be taken aside as a group (possibly in a homogeneous class labeled *General, Basic, Service, Essential, Opportunity,* or *Second-Track*) and given a greater opportunity as a group to learn rules which teachers assume would have guided these students to better performance on such tests. It is fairly common for the teacher of such a group to spend up to a semester or more on the formal study of grammar alone. The aims are to teach certain rules, to teach what is described by the rules, and to teach students how to recognize "correct" or "incorrect" word forms and syntax which are symbolized by the labels and described by the rules.

Because many of these students have done poorly in grammar and usage, the teacher often assumes that it is wise to start with the basic elements, the parts of speech, even in the upper years of senior high. A grammar book, a workbook with review exercises, and dittoed or mimeographed exercises and tests prepared by the teacher or by other teachers are the major teaching materials. Rules are reviewed and retaught, and sentences are scanned for errors. Words and word groups are underlined or diagramed and given labels. Students restate rules on tests to prove that they have been guided by these statements in making judgments about correctness.

Plan II does not assume that students must be homogeneously grouped; in some respects the plan might be aided by homogeneous grouping, but it can be used in schools that are too small to permit grouping. The teacher examines all evidence of poor performance on departmental tests and standardized tests but is not satisfied with this evidence alone. At the beginning of the semester, he asks for several short pieces of writing ranging from a sentence to a paragraph (written in class and turned in before the end of the period) and notes weaknesses in grammar and usage. In doing so, he distinguishes between gross errors and disputable items just below the skirts of formality. He listens to the speech of his students and perhaps tapes it in informal and formal situations. This information, together with the results of a comprehensive diagnostic test, is placed on individual record forms, charts, or profiles which the students keep as records of their individual progress.

With this information in hand, the teacher and his students draw upon a wide range of resources to prompt study and use of the language. Students may also work with programed materials which present "reinforced knowledge" inductively and individually. In "programed" study and in small-group instruction and individual or group substitution drills in usage, the teacher will begin with individual weaknesses which are the most serious.

Much emphasis is placed on reinforcement through *performance*. In other words, the teacher does not take even a perfect score on a programed exercise as proof that the student knows something well enough to use it in expressing himself. In an immediate follow-up to an inductive lesson, students are led to use their own words in building sentences which contain the appropriate usage and improved syntax which they have just studied inductively. As a next step, students often compare their sentences with ones written by classmates who have completed the same lessons and have followed the same directions for building sentences. The teacher also supplies a number of model sentences for comparison.

After the teacher teaches an inductive lesson or after students complete independent study, the teacher looks particularly for evidence of improvement in the specifics taught in these ways. Realizing this, students expect the teacher, probably in a laboratory-type writing lesson, to examine papers in class for evidence of improvement in something just taught or just studied independently. Lack of improvement may justify asking a student to branch into an alternate programed lesson for added reinforcement, holding a conference with him, or teaching the point inductively to him or to a group of others who indicate repeatedly that they have the same problem.

In summary, what does Plan II assume can be accomplished? The teacher diagnoses each student's individual weaknesses and allows him to concentrate on them in the order of their seriousness, thus eliminating much of the useless repetition which subjects a class to instruction needed by only a few. The students have opportunities to apply knowledge in building original sentences. Evaluation is narrowed to the specific kinds of improvement which individuals are trying to make. Individual profiles and progress charts give students a look at their own improvement, and these are passed to the next grade where the students will be given further opportunities to overcome their individual weaknesses in knowledge and use of the language.

Is Plan II too idealistic, or even impossible? Where is the time, and where are the teaching materials to do such a thing? Perhaps time can be provided by taking a hard look at present practices in literature, language, and composition. Are three-minute oral book reports day after day really as helpful as imagined? Must the discussion of a long work be held up by the assignment of a chapter or a scene at a time? Do some works deserve three or four weeks of study? Must some thematic units be so broad? Must every selection in the anthology be studied or even read? Must the same points in grammar and usage be taught and reviewed year after year? If the teacher is unwilling to give up doing these things, new instructional materials may provide a way of individualizing instruction while the usual units and lessons are taught. There are materials which a student can use independently; he learns by himself and charts his own progress. In composition there is the new *Writing Skills Laboratory* published by Science Research Associates, and in grammar and usage there is *Individualized English* published by Follett Company. Programed books and transparencies are also available for individual and group study. Other kinds of materials, such as taped exercises for oral practices and critical listening, will follow soon, and it also seems likely that some of these will be designed for individualized instruction. Key steps in using all such materials will very likely be diagnostic testing, individualized self-instruction, trial performance, and post-testing of points included in diagnostic testing. Individual records will be kept and passed on as part of the cumulative records of individual progress and achievement.

A CONFESSION AND A CHALLENGE

Urged forward by the promise of new developments in literature, composition, and language, the English teaching profession has tended to overlook the fact that its teachers must have valid and reliable instruments to use in assessing the changes that may result from applying new theories and new teaching tools in the classroom. Even researchers, funded heavily under government contracts, are tempted to believe that existing instruments will measure expected change. One fact may not be very clear: new theories, new methods, and new tools have outdistanced tests and measurement in English. A significant trend that connects all others is the growing belief by scholars that the teaching of English is both a respectable and a highly interesting subject for scholarly and scientific inquiry. But scholars in English and in English education still do not want to study testing and measurement. If their reluctance stems from romantic notions that nothing significant in English can be tested, they should consider the therapeutic value of a confession to this way of thinking.

Traditional ways of assessing change are still valuable, but they fall short of giving teachers much information. Traditional tests can extract from a student his accumulation of new facts, his knowledge of how his subject is described and structured, his knowledge of generalizations that other people have formed about the subject, even restatements of his own generalization. But these kinds of responses all constitute a rehash. The new method described elsewhere in this book can be used to free the teacher and the student *to think in the subject*. Applied to classroom research and teaching, the new method creates an immediate need for instruments that will assess a student's method of inquiry in the subject; his ability to arrive at his own generalizations about literature, composition, and language; and his ability to *use* these generalizations in personally receiving, evaluating, ordering, and communicating ideas.

The challenge to teachers and professional testmakers should be obvious. The spirit of inquiry and creation which has led to new developments in English must lead the way to new ways of assessing change. Teachers must not wait for professional test-makers to create tests or to tell teachers how to create them. Because English teachers are the persons most responsible for assessing change, they must develop whatever instruments they believe will do the job, no matter how far-fetched these instruments may seem at first to them or to other persons. The time-honored distrust of experts in tests and measurements is now mainly a fictitious barrier to interdisciplinary efforts in assessment; leaders in tests and measurements today welcome the challenge of finding the statistics needed for appropriate and helpful analyses of promising teacher-made tests.

SELECTED REFERENCES

Buros, O. K. *The Sixth Mental Measurements Yearbook.* Highland Park, New Jersey: Gryphon Press, 1965.
————. *Tests in Print.* Highland Park, New Jersey: Gryphon Press, 1961.
Burton, Dwight L. "Approaches to Ranges of Ability." *Literature Study in the High Schools.* New York: Holt, Rinehart and Winston, Inc., 1964. Pp. 273-93.
Carruthers, Robert. *Building Better English Tests.* Champaign, Illinois: National Council of Teachers of English, 1963.
Chauncey, Henry, and John E. Dobbin. *Testing: Its Place in Education Today.* New York: Harper & Row, 1963.
Commission on the Curriculum of the National Council of Teachers of English. "A Check List for Evaluating the English Program in the Junior and Senior High School." *The English Journal,* LI (April, 1962), 273-82.
Corbin, Richard. "Evaluating the Reading and Study of Poetry." *The English Journal,* XLVI (March, 1957), 154-57.
Diedrich, P. *Short-Cut Statistics for Teacher-Made Tests.* Evaluation and Advisory Service Series, No. 5. Princeton, New Jersey: Educational Testing Service, 1960.
Durost, Walter N., and G. A. Prescott. *Essentials of Measurement for Teachers.* New York: Harcourt, Brace & World, 1962.
Dusel, William J. "Some Semantic Implications of Theme Cor-

rection." *The English Journal,* XLIV (October, 1955), 390-97.

Ebel, Robert L. *Measuring Educational Achievement.* Englewood Cliffs, New Jersey: Prentice-Hall, Inc., 1965.

Edwards, Allen L. *Techniques of Attitude Scale & Construction.* New York: Appleton-Century-Crofts, 1957.

Evans, William H, ed. *Testing in English. Illinois English Bulletin,* LII (February, 1965).

Gardner, Eric F. "Development and Applications of Tests of Educational Achievement in Schools and Colleges." *Review of Educational Research,* XXIII (February, 1953), 85-101.

Gordon, Edward J. "Levels of Teaching and Testing." *The English Journal,* XLIV (September, 1955), 330-34.

Green, J. A. *Teacher-Made Tests.* New York: Harper & Row, 1963.

Gronlund, Norman. *Measurement and Evaluation in Teaching.* New York: The Macmillan Company, 1965.

Harris, Chester W. *Problems in Measuring Change.* Madison: University of Wisconsin Press, 1963.

Judine, Sister M., I.H.M., ed. *A Guide for Evaluating Student Composition.* Champaign, Illinois: The National Council of Teachers of English, 1965.

Koclanes, T. A. "Can We Evaluate Compositions?" *The English Journal,* L (April, 1961), 252-57 ff.

Loban, Walter. "Evaluating Growth in the Study of Literature." *The English Journal,* XXXVII (June, 1948), 277-83.

Lowe, Lee Frank. "Theme Correction via Tape Recorder." *The English Journal,* LII (March, 1963), 212-14.

Lumsden, Robert. "Dictation Machines as Teacher Aids." *The English Journal,* L (November, 1961), 555-56.

McKey, Eleanor. "Do Standardized Tests Do What They Claim to Do?" *The English Journal,* L (December, 1961), 607-11.

National Society for the Study of Education, Sixty-Second Yearbook, Part II. *The Impact and Improvement of School Testing Programs.* Chicago: University of Chicago Press, 1964.

Palmer, Orville. "Seven Classic Ways of Grading Dishonestly." *The English Journal,* LI (October, 1962), 464-67.

Perrine, Laurence. "The Nature of Proof in the Interpretation of

Poetry." *The English Journal,* LI (September, 1962), 393-98.

Pooley, Robert C. "The Evaluation of Grammar Teaching." *Teaching English Grammar.* Chapter 14. New York: Appleton-Century-Crofts, Inc., 1957. Pp. 181-202.

Reid, James M. "An Adventure in Programing Literature." *The English Journal,* LII (December, 1963), 659-73.

Sanders, Norris M. *Classroom Questions.* New York: Harper & Row, 1966.

Smith, Fred M., and Sam Adams. *Educational Measurement for the Classroom Teacher.* New York: Harper & Row, 1966.

Steinberg, E. R., E. Fenton, G. A. Forehand, and R. C. Slack. *Curriculum Development and Evaluation in English and Social Studies.* Cooperative Research Project No. F-041. Pittsburgh: Carnegie Institute of Technology, 1964.

Sterling, Edna. "Evaluating Growth in Language." *The English Journal,* XXXVII (April, 1948), 240-44.

Travers, Robert M. W. *How to Make Achievement Tests.* New York: The Odyssey Press, Inc., 1950.

Tyler, Fred T., and Walter R. Stellwagen. "The Search for Evidence About Individual Differences." *Individualizing Instruction.* The Sixty-First Yearbook, Part II. Chicago: The National Society for the Study of Education, 1962. Pp. 95-111.

Upton, Albert, and Richard W. Samson. *Creative Analysis.* New York: E. P. Dutton and Co., Inc., 1963.

Wood, Dorothy A. *Test Construction.* Columbus, Ohio: Charles E. Merrill Books, 1960.

VII

New Trends
in Teacher Education

Soaring enrollments in the secondary schools have caused the greatest shortage of English teachers in the history of the nation. But the problem is more complicated than meeting a teacher shortage with the needed number of teachers. To new developments in English and the teaching of English must be added a rapidly expanding range of abilities and backgrounds in the student population, and an overriding concern for academic excellence. Caught between the need for teachers with superior knowledge and skills and the need to fill vacancies, many schools face a dilemma. Frequently a choice must be made between an applicant with weak academic and professional preparation and one with a fairly strong academic background but with little professional skill or dedication. Both kinds of background are undesirable. To eliminate the dilemma and meet the challenge of new developments at the same time, the profession must do at least two things: it must meet an unprecedented teacher shortage with an unprecedented number of teachers with unprecedented competencies, and it must move exceedingly fast with programs of re-education and continuing education. The second responsibility is by *no means* second in importance. A young English teacher who entered the classroom in 1960 could, without re-education, become an anachronism by 1970.

Assuming leadership in meeting the problems of teacher preparation in English, the National Council of Teachers of English established in 1958 its Commission on the Profession, which sponsored special workshops on teacher education. By 1964, NCTE had completed four expansive projects: (1) The Committee on National Interest conducted a nationwide survey of the status of the profession and revealed its findings in a publication entitled *The National Interest and the Teaching of English* (1961); (2) The NCTE Commission on the English Curriculum terminated its activities in 1963 with the publication of *The Education of Teachers of English for American Schools and Colleges;* (3) The Committee on Methods Courses in Teaching of English at the Secondary Level conducted a nationwide survey and published its findings in *Specialized Courses in Methods of Teaching English* (1964); (4) The Committee on National Interest conducted another massive survey and reported its data in *The National Interest and the Continuing Education of Teachers of English* (1964).

THE SHAPE OF THINGS

As the teaching of English in the secondary schools moved into the present decade, a fact long suspected was discovered through research and addressed to the Congress of the United States and the United States Office of Education. Over half of the secondary teachers teaching English were woefully unprepared to teach the subject.[1] The full import of this inadequacy cannot be ascertained, but the specter looms large indeed. Here are some facts gathered in a survey of the preparatory programs in 374 colleges offering major work in English:

Only a fourth of the colleges require a course in the history of the English language.

Only 17.4 per cent require a course in modern English grammar.

Fewer than 200 are graduating teachers of English informed about modern language study.

Only 41 per cent require a course in advanced composition.

More than 50 per cent require 18 to 24 semester hours in literature.

[1] The following data have been summarized from *The National Interest and the Teaching of English* (Champaign, Illinois: National Council of Teachers of English, 1961). Reprinted by permission of the Council.

More than two-thirds require courses in English literature, American literature, and Shakespeare; only one-third require work in world literature.

Only one-fifth specify the need for a course in contemporary literature or in literary criticism or critical analysis.

Few institutions provide for the study of literature written for adolescents.

Only 51.5 per cent require a course in methods of teaching English.

In methods courses, more time is spent on the teaching of literature than on the teaching of grammar and the teaching of composition combined.

Considering that only one-half of 7,417 practicing teachers of English who answered another survey had college majors in English,[2] the profession must view with alarm these facts about their continuing education:

Two-thirds of the 7,417 surveyed do not consider themselves well prepared to teach composition and oral skills; 90 per cent do not consider themselves well prepared to teach reading; almost 50 per cent do not consider themselves well prepared to teach literature and language.

43.9 per cent rarely or never take courses during the evening; 17.2 per cent rarely or never take summer courses; 70.6 per cent rarely or never take courses on weekends.

90 per cent never or rarely have an opportunity to take a sabbatical leave.

30.4 per cent have not taken a course in English for more than 10 years; 27.7 per cent have not completed any education courses.

Three-fifths have never had an opportunity to confer with a college professor of English, a college specialist in English education, or a special English supervisor.

Only one-third are often able to confer with a librarian or with fellow English teachers.

29.3 per cent never have an opportunity to attend a workshop or institute sponsored by a school district.

[2]From *The Continuing Education of Teachers of English* (Champaign, Illinois: National Council of Teachers of English, 1964). Reprinted by permission of the Council.

23.6 per cent never attend local professional meetings of English teachers; 48.8 per cent never attend state meetings; 82.1 per cent never attend national meetings.

EMERGING PROFILES IN
TEACHER QUALIFICATION

The profiles discovered by NCTE researchers must not be the profiles of tomorrow. The demands for new knowledge and for special skills in teaching English have risen so sharply that an undergraduate with thirty-two or thirty-six semester hours in the subject may very soon have insufficient preparation for student teaching. This prospect has caused some persons responsible for teacher preparation at the undergraduate level to consider abolishing the teaching minor in a second teaching field in order to provide a major in literature and a minor in linguistics and written composition.

In recognition of the apparent inadequacy of preservice preparation at the undergraduate level, some states grant only a provisional certificate to a high school teacher until the teacher completes further college work, usually at the graduate level. Some school systems make it clear to a teacher at the time of his employment that he must earn a master's degree within five years in order to continue in the system. Other systems do not want to discuss employment with a candidate who does not have a master's degree.

With or without certain courses, with or without degrees, the major consideration should be the competencies — knowledge and skills — possessed by the candidate. Recently, several profiles of competencies have appeared. The question of whether all of these competencies are equally important in teaching English in the secondary schools should be tested by research. Perhaps proficiency examinations, major revisions in existing courses, tutorials, and clinical experiences will strengthen programs without adding courses. Perhaps a certain number of new courses will be needed. These assumptions must be tested as well.

The two profiles which follow are based on assumptions. They are statements of competencies which leaders in the teaching of

English feel should compose the profile of the secondary school English teacher; as such, they become extremely important guidelines in making changes in curriculum and in creating instruments to measure subsequent changes in a teacher's behavior in the classroom.

PROFILE A

The following list was prepared by the Committee on the National Interest and is printed here with permission of the National Council of Teachers of English.

A Standard of Preparation to Teach English[3]

I. The teacher of English should have a certain fundamental and specialized knowledge of the English language and its literature, together with certain abilities and skills which enable him to perform expertly in his discipline.

A. In language, he should have:

1. A fundamental knowledge of the historical development and present character of the English language: phonology (phonetics and phonemics), morphology, syntax, vocabulary (etymology and semantics), the relations of language and society.

2. A specialized knowledge of the English language which is appropriate to the teacher's particular field of interest and responsibility.

3. An informed command of the arts of language— rhetoric and logic; ability to speak and write language which is not only unified, coherent, and correct but also responsible, appropriate to the situation, and stylistically effective.

B. In literature, he should have:

1. A reading background of major literary works which emphasize the essential dignity of the individual man. This background:

a. Implies a knowledge of major works, writers, forms, themes, and movements of the literature of the English-speaking people.

b. Reflects intensive study of many literary pieces.

c. Includes familiarity with some of the outstanding literary works in English translation, or in the original language, of the Greek, Roman,

[3]*The National Interest and the Teaching of English,* pp. 40-42.

Norse, Italian, French, Spanish, German, Slavic, and Oriental peoples.

2. A specialized knowledge of whatever writers and literary works, forms, themes, media, and movements are appropriate to the teacher's particular field of interest and responsibility.

3. An ability to analyze and evaluate independently the various forms of imaginative literature as well as the utilitarian forms of verbal expression, and the insight to use suitable critical approaches in order to discover their literary and human values.

II. The teacher of English should have certain abilities and knowledge which belong to the science and the art of teaching language and literature.

A. These abilities include:

1. The ability to envision how his students may develop their potentialities through the study of language and literature.

2. The ability to excite their interest and direct their learning.

3. The ability to help them understand and use English practically and creatively.

4. The ability to elevate their taste and critical powers.

5. The ability to lead them to a perception of human problems and an appreciation of human values.

6. The ability to evaluate their progress and the efficacy of his own methods.

B. These abilities presuppose not only the fundamental but also the specialized knowledge and skills of the English language and literature which the teacher needs to fulfill his professional responsibility.

C. These abilities imply knowledge of the philosophies of education and the psychologies of learning as they relate to the study and teaching of the English language and its literature. Such knowledge:

1. Reveals how an individual unfolds and grows through his use and understanding of language and literature.

2. Supplies the teacher with a variety of methods for use in teaching his students the skills and arts which are appropriate to their level of attainment in English.

3. Informs the teacher of the relation which each phase or level has to the total school, college, and university program.

4. Includes an awareness of the basic issues in the teaching of English.

PROFILE B

The following background information and lists have been printed with permission of the Illinois State-Wide Curriculum Study Center in the Preparation of Secondary School English Teachers, which is funded by a research contract with the United States Office of Education and directed by Professor J. N. Hook, English Department, University of Illinois.[4]

Qualifications of Secondary School Teachers of English:

A Preliminary Statement

The Illinois State-wide Curriculum Study Center in the Preparation of Secondary School English Teachers (ISCPET) is supported by funds supplied in accordance with a contract with the U. S. Office of Education. Representatives of the twenty institutions[5] involved in ISCPET are conducting a five-year study of ways of improving teacher preparation. They have prepared as a working guide the preliminary lists of qualifications that follow. The representatives, drawn from departments of English and Education, base this statement upon their own experience and observation; upon the recommendations of an advisory committee composed of twelve nationally known persons in English, Speech, and Education; and upon additional recommendations from Illinois authorities on certification, school administrators, secondary school English consultants, English department heads; and English teachers.

The lists have these five headings: Knowledge of Lan-

[4]Another study of teacher preparation in English is the English Teacher Preparation Study, which is cooperatively sponsored by the National Association of State Directors of Teacher Education and Certification, the National Council of Teachers of English, and the Modern Language Association of America. Funded by a USOE research contract and directed by William P. Viall, School of Education, Western Michigan University, this study developed written guidelines for the preparation of teachers of English in the secondary schools and for that portion of the program for elementary teachers which relates to the teaching of English. Unlike the ISCPET study, the NASDTEC-MLA-NCTE study does not test assumptions through research.

[5]The twenty institutions: Aurora College, Bradley University, DePaul University, Greenville College, Illinois Institute of Technology, Illinois State University at Normal, Illinois Wesleyan University, Knox College, Loyola University, Monmouth College, North Central College, Northwestern University, Olivet Nazarene College, Rockford College, Roosevelt University, St. Xavier College, Southern Illinois University, University of Chicago, University of Illinois (Champaign-Urbana Campus), Western Illinois University.

guage; Knowledge and Skill in Written Composition; Knowledge and Skill in Literature; Knowledge and Skill in Oral Communication; and Knowledge and Skill in the Teaching of English.

Although no specific list of competencies in general education has been prepared, there is a consensus that any teacher of English should possess at least basic knowledge of social science, natural science, and the humanities other than English, including at least a fair command of a foreign language. No attempt has been made to list the personal qualities that are involved in successful teaching. Such a list, incorporating as it must such varied items as integrity, willingness to work hard, liking for children, and a pleasant voice, would be little more than a catalog of virtues desirable in any human being.

The division into five lists has been for the sake of coherence in presentation. Such separation is admittedly artificial. For example, competencies in language, literature, and compostion are in truth inseparable; professional and academic qualifications necessarily interact.

Persons responsible for planning college curriculums based upon the competencies must realize that no one-to-one ratio exists between competencies and courses. That is, the attainment of one competency may require more than one college course, and conversely, a single course may sometimes provide sufficient instruction to cover several of the competencies.

In these lists, the "minimal" level of qualification describes the competencies to be expected of a secondary school English teacher who has no more than a teaching minor in English. It may, however, also describe the competencies of an English major whose ability is only mediocre or whose college preparation has been of less than average quality.

The "good" level of qualification describes competencies reasonable to expect in able or fairly able English majors whose ability and college preparation have been average or better in quality.

The "superior" level of qualification describes competencies to be expected in highly able persons whose college preparation has been of very good or excellent quality; it is likely to include graduate work and may require some years of teaching experience.

The "minimal" qualifications are not recommended. Rather, they are basic to attaining the "good" qualifications. Each college or university engaged in preparing secondary school teachers of English should, in the opinion of those responsible for this report, attempt to prepare teachers who have attained at least the "good" level.

Qualifications of Secondary School Teachers of English

1. Knowledge of Language

Minimal	Good	Superior
An understanding of how language functions	A detailed understanding of how language functions, including knowledge of the principles of semantics	
A reasonably detailed knowledge of one system of English grammar and a working familiarity with another system	A detailed knowledge of at least two systems of English grammar	
A knowledge of the present standards of educated usage; knowledge of the various levels of usage and how those levels are determined	A thorough knowledge of levels of usage; some knowledge of dialectology; a realization of the cultural implications of both	Sufficient knowledge to illustrate richly and specifically the areas listed under "good"
	A knowledge of the history of the English language, with appropriate awareness of its phonological, morphological and syntactic changes	

2. Knowledge and Skill in Written Composition

Minimal	Good	Superior
Ability to recognize such characteristics of good writing as substantial and relevant content; organization; clarity; appropriateness of tone; and accuracy in mechanics and usage	A well-developed ability to recognize such characteristics of good writing as substantial and relevant content; organization; clarity; appropriateness of tone; and accuracy in mechanics and usage	In addition to "good" competencies, a detailed knowledge of theories and history of rhetoric and of the development of English prose
A basic understanding of the processes of composing	Perception of the complexities in the processes of composing	Perception of the subtleties, as well as the complexities, in the

Qualifications of Secondary School Teachers of English (Continued)

		processes of composing
Ability to analyze and to communicate to students the specific strengths and weaknesses in their writing	Ability to analyze in detail the strengths and weaknesses in the writing of students and to communicate the analysis effectively	Ability to give highly perceptive analysis of the strengths and weaknesses in the writing of students, to communicate this exactly, and to motivate students toward greater and greater strengths
Ability to produce writing with at least a modicum of the characteristics noted above	Proficiency in producing writing with at least considerable strength in the characteristics noted above	Proficiency in producing writing of genuine power; ability and willingness to write for publication

3. Knowledge and Skill in Literature

Minimal	Good	Superior
Acquaintance with the most important works of major English and American authors	Familiarity with the important works of major English and American authors; knowledge of the characteristics of various genres and of major works in English and American literature in the genres	In addition to the "good" competencies: Intensive and extensive knowledge of one or more major authors and of at least one genre, and one period; knowledge of major works of selected foreign writers, both ancient and modern, and of comparative literature
Awareness of the patterns of development of English and American literature from their beginnings to the present	As part of the awareness of patterns of development, a knowledge of such backgrounds of English and American literature as history, the Bible, mythology, and folklore	
Ability to read closely an unfamiliar literary text of average difficulty with compre-	Ability to read closely an unfamiliar literary text of above-average difficulty with good	Familiarity with major critical theories and schools of criticism

Qualifications of Secondary School Teachers of English (Continued)

hension of its content and salient literary characteristics	comprehension of its content and literary characteristics
	Familiarity with a considerable body of literature suitable for adolescents

4. Knowledge and Skill in Oral Communication

Minimal	Good	Superior
An understanding of basic principles of preparing and presenting an oral report	An understanding of the principles of group discussion, group dynamics, oral reporting, panel discussions, classroom dramatizations, and choral reading; an understanding of the relationships between speaking and other facets of English	In addition to the "good" competencies: touches of expertise and showmanship that a professional speaker, oral interpreter, or actor possesses
An awareness of the role of listening in communication	A knowledge of current information relative to listening techniques	
An ability to speak with clarity and in conformity with present standards of educated usage	An ability to speak clearly and effectively, and in conformity with present standards of educated usage	
An ability to read aloud well enough for ready comprehension	An ability to read aloud well enough to convey most aspects of the interpretive art—meaning, mood, dominant emotions, varying emotions, overtones, and variety	

Qualifications of Secondary School Teachers of English (Continued)

5. Knowledge and Skill in the Teaching of English

Minimal	Good	Superior
Some understanding of basic principles of educational psychology	Knowledge of educational psychology, especially of the learning process and adolescent psychology	Competence in the knowledge and application of educational psychology; detailed knowledge of the stages of language growth in children and youth
Introductory knowledge of American secondary education	Knowledge of the philosophy, organization, and educational programs of American secondary education now and in historical perspective	
A basic understanding of the content, instructional materials, and organization of secondary English programs	A good understanding of the content, instructional materials, and organization of secondary English programs, and of the role of English in the total school program	A thorough understanding of the content, instructional materials, and organization of secondary English programs, and of the role of English in the total school program; knowledge of principles of curriculum development in English
A basic knowledge of ways to teach English, with an awareness of the importance of developing assignments that guide students in their study of language, written and oral communication, and literature	A wide knowledge of effective ways to teach English, to select and adapt methods and materials for the varying interests and maturity levels of students, and to develop a sequence of assignments to guide and	A thorough knowledge of the most effective ways to teach English, to select and adapt methods and materials for the varying interests and maturity levels of students, and to develop sequential assignments

Qualifications of Secondary School Teachers of English (Continued)

	stimulate students in their study of language, written and oral communication, and literature	that guide, stimulate, and challenge students in their study of language, written and oral communication, and literature
Some knowledge of corrective and developmental reading techniques	Moderate knowledge of corrective and developmental reading techniques	A relatively thorough knowledge of corrective and developmental reading techniques
Understanding of basic principles of evaluation and test construction in English	Broad understanding of basic principles of evaluation and test construction in English	Thorough understanding of basic principles of evaluation and test construction in English

Source: Illinois State-Wide Curriculum Study Center in the Preparation of Secondary School English Teachers.

A NEW PROFILE IN TEACHER PREPARATION[6]

In the academic year 1965-66, the School of Education at Northwestern University, in cooperation with representatives of other areas of study, instituted its Tutorial and Clinical Program of teacher education. This program assumes that a well-prepared teacher needs to have (1) a broad general education, (2) a control in depth of the content of one or more teaching fields, (3) study in the foundations of education, (4) continuous exposure to schools and school children throughout the four years of the undergraduate career, and (5) training in appropriate teaching skills and methods of organizing material to be taught.

Northwestern University's General Education courses, required of all undergraduates, are basic to the new program and

[6]This section is based upon a description submitted by Sidney R. Berquist, Assistant Professor of Education, Northwestern University, Evanston, Illinois. The project is supported by a grant under the Carnegie Foundation. Since the program was instituted with freshmen in 1965-66, it will not be completed for several years.

comprise four of the twelve quarters of work leading to the bachelor's degree. Four quarters of work in subject-matter content, through the development of a major concentration in one or more of the departments of the School of Arts and Sciences, are also required.

Students in the Tutorial and Clinical Program do not enroll in formal courses in professional education. Upon electing this program the student is assigned to a tutorial professor who directs him through the four years in an individualized schedule of seminars, readings, lectures, and independent study in the theoretical foundations of education. Concurrent clinical experiences engage the student in a variety of activities in cooperating public schools and community service organizations. The clinical experiences are under the direct supervision of jointly appointed professors of education who are also active teachers in the public schools. These clinical professors hold half-time appointments in both the cooperating school districts and in the School of Education at Northwestern University.

Each student follows a sequenced program of study in professional education that starts in the fall quarter of his freshman year. In the winter and spring quarters of this year he studies, with his tutorial professor, some of the persistent issues and problems in American education — political, social, moral, ethical, and legal. Through a series of seminars, lectures, and outside readings, the student comes in contact with pressing issues in modern education. Coordinate clinical experiences are designed to expose the prospective teacher to the context of these issues and questions through a number of visits to schools that represent a wide range of programs and community backgrounds. During the spring quarter, the student also has an opportunity to engage in dialogues with the personnel of these schools and to come in direct contact with pupils. For one-half day a week, he is also engaged in voluntary services, perhaps in a hospital, in a nursery school, or with an after-school tutoring project.

The projected plan of studies for the sophomore year concentrates on the foundations of education — sociological, historical, philosophical, and psychological. In tutorial seminars and discussions the student considers the social structures and environments of the schools as well as historical and philosophical bases for current school practices. He also works one-half day a week as a teacher aide under the direct supervision of a clinical professor in an elementary or junior high school. Clinical experiences span several grade levels within the school and serve as a clinical laboratory for the description and identification of the social structures of the school. These schools also serve as sites for observations of individual children carried out in connection with other course work in educational psychology.

During his junior year, the student concentrates on developing his competencies as a teacher. During tutorial sessions—consisting of lectures, seminars and workshops—he examines goals for teaching, the general problems of choosing appropriate content to teach, and the principles of curriculum design. In September he starts his clinical experiences with two or three weeks of classroom observation. Through the rest of the year, one-half day a week, he continues as an assistant to a teacher in his subject field. Thus, the prospective teacher concentrates in the tutorials on planning for teaching. In his clinical experiences he becomes successively more involved in the act of teaching.

During the fall and winter quarters of the senior year, students in the program are separated into groups according to their chosen subject fields. In the tutorials they concentrate on a study of the research findings and principles of presentation in their fields. This study proceeds under the joint direction of the tutorial professors and subject-matter teaching specialists on the faculty of Northwestern University. During the fall quarter, seniors return to the same schools they visited in the junior year. Again they work with clinical professors for two or three more weeks in September and for one-half day a week on a continuing basis. At this time, the prospective teacher is encouraged to take more responsibility for teaching. During the winter quarter, he is phased into full-time student teaching. Actual student teaching time is variable, from two to eight weeks or more, depending on the needs of the student for classroom practice at this time. Clinical and tutorial seminars, coordinated with student teaching, enable the student to study such things as grouping and grading practices in the school context.

The spring quarter of the senior year is largely devoted to the writing of a senior thesis, a paper of substantial length in the student's teaching field. Each student writes this thesis under the joint direction of a tutorial and clinical professor, using experimental and factual data from his clinical experiences.

Evaluation of the Clinical and Tutorial Program, which is aided and coordinated by a research director assigned to the staff, is the continuing responsibility of all personnel in the program. The students are being compared in performance and attitude with prospective teachers in the traditional training program, and on certain factors with a cross-section of all undergraduates at the university. The evaluation project will follow all groups of students through their undergraduate years and into their first years after graduation.

The significant features of this program for the preparation of English teachers center on the breadth and quality of the experiences the student will have. Main features may be summarized as follows:

Each student takes the same course work in English, totaling sixty quarter hours (forty-five semester hours), required of all undergraduate majors in the English department. Each student may also elect two full quarters of academic work in English or a supporting field.

Each student prepares for teaching with practicing specialists in his field of concentration. Tutorial professors and other faculty at Northwestern are also active researchers in education and in the teaching of English. Clinical professors are practicing teachers of English in the secondary schools.

Each student has contact with children of all ages, from preschool through high school, both in and out of the school setting. For example, the prospective teacher of secondary school English will have first-hand knowledge of the language development of nursery school and elementary school children through his contacts as an observer and as an assistant teacher.

Each student has the opportunity and the responsibility to apply his studies in the foundations of education and the theory of teaching of English to the immediate demands of children learning in the classroom.

Although the Tutorial and Clinical Program in Teacher Education at Northwestern University is only in its inception, it gives promise of producing knowledgeable, balanced teachers of

English who will be able to assume positions of leadership in the profession.

RECENT DEVELOPMENTS
IN CONTINUING EDUCATION

Although continuing education is not advancing as rapidly or as dramatically as preservice preparation, two points can be made with some optimism: significant progress has already been made in the continuing education of English teachers, and the potential for unparalleled expansion now exists. Many school systems are apparently helping to defray expenses of English teachers who attend professional meetings and conventions. A survey taken of the more than nine thousand English teachers in attendance at the 1965 NCTE convention revealed that 80 per cent had their expenses paid in part or in full by educational institutions or school systems. More school systems are organizing in-service workshops and requesting extension classes. Foundations are helping to set up in-service programs. The Martha Holden Jennings Foundation of the Greater Cleveland area has brought in outstanding educators to speak to teachers. The Esso Foundation of Baltimore has set up in-service programs in linguistics and humanities. Local and state school systems have employed English supervisors to aid in building and coordinating programs, in translating new developments into workable classroom practice, and in furthering the education of practicing teachers.[7]

The greatest potential for in-service education may lie in the inclusion of English in the National Defense Education Act, and in the opportunities available through the Elementary and Secondary Education Act of 1965 and the Higher Education Act of 1965. Under Title Eleven of NDEA, professors of English and English education cooperatively instructed thousands of English teachers who attended 103 English Institutes in the

[7]Sue M. Brett, ed., *Supervision of English, Grades K-12: A Resource Book for State and Local School Systems* (Champaign, Illinois: National Council of Teachers of English, 1965). For the English chairman's role in the secondary school see Robert J. LaCampagne, ed. *High School Departments of English: Their Organization, Administration, and Supervision* (Champaign, Illinois: National Council of Teachers of English, 1965).

summer of 1965. One hundred twenty-seven English Institutes were held during the summer of 1966, including one specifically for secondary English supervisors and department heads. Thus, the scope of institute programs has already extended far beyond the pioneering programs of the National Council of Teachers of English and the rather extensive programs of the College Entrance Examination Board. Under Title Three of NDEA, English teachers are able to purchase supplementary teaching materials and equipment for as little as half-price. Knowing that they can receive such teaching resources at a reduced cost if they can show how the materials will aid in the improvement of their programs, more teachers are working together to find ways to strengthen their programs. Teachers will, of course, learn much in the process. The Elementary and Secondary Education Act of 1965 is encouraging both in-service learning and additional college training. As a definite link to the colleges, the Higher Education Act of 1965 provides financial assistance to teachers seeking graduate coursework and advanced degrees.

THE GROWING COMMITMENT

In a very few years, the English profession has greatly strengthened its commitment to the teaching of English. History was made in 1958 when English professors met with persons from other disciplines and acknowledged teacher preparation as a respectable topic for study and inquiry. The occasion was a series of meetings on "The Basic Issues in the Teaching of English," and those in attendance represented the American Studies Association, the College English Association, the Modern Language Association, and the National Council of Teachers of English. In January, 1962, Project English began under the United States Office of Education's cooperative research program. The same year, college English department chairmen from across the nation met at Allerton Park, Illinois, and drafted resolutions concerning the preparation and continuing education of English teachers. Also in 1962, scholars and teachers, psychologists, administrators, and representatives of educational organizations concerned with the teaching of English at all levels assembled for a Project English Research Conference on Needed Research in the Teaching of English. In 1963, leaders in English, English education, psychology, and tests and measurements met at New York University for the Research Development Seminar in the Teaching of English. Later in 1963, a larger group of specialists in several disciplines held the San Francisco Conference on Research Design in the Teaching of English.

All of these developments were milestones, but none was as history-making or as significant as the first national Conference on English Education, which attracted over two hundred specialists in English and English Education to the Indiana University campus in March, 1963. The high interest and the constructive suggestions that characterized this conference supported the assumption that "the conflict between the liberal arts and professional education is a spurious one and that quality teacher education represents a sound blend of the liberal and professional components."[8]

After this highly successful conference, the formation two years later of the Conference on English Education as a professional organization came as no surprise to persons interested in the teaching of English. Composed of virtually every leader in the teaching of English, this organization could become the nation's greatest single force in solving the dilemmas confronting education in English at all levels.

THE LIFE CYCLE

Influential as the Conference on English Education will be as a national organization, it obviously cannot overcome all problems. Who else, then, is responsible for teacher preparation in English? Who else can become a force for improvement? The emergence of the superior English teacher depends in great measure upon the workings of a very complicated image-making life cycle which has at least four phases.

Phase One can be called the early environment of the would-be

[8]Dwight L. Burton, ed., *English Education Today* (Champaign, Illinois: National Council of Teachers of English, 1963), p. 9.

teacher. In this phase, the promising college-bound adolescent who is beginning to consider what he would like to do some day becomes aware of the image of the English teacher in the eyes of parents and the community in general. The adolescent is likely to have some questions. Is the English teacher understood and respected, or is this person stereotyped as a low-income "comma hound," usually a woman? What is the image of the English teacher in the eyes of other students? Does the teacher inspire even the boys to consider the teaching of English? And what of the image of the English teacher in the eyes of other English teachers and school administrators? Do English teachers speak out for themselves and seem proud of their profession? Do administrators seem to respect good work in English? Do they recognize it publically?

Phase Two is the college environment of the would-be teacher. The image of the high school English teacher fades, and the student looks for new images in his contacts with college professors. New questions emerge. Does the English professor inspire the student with his teaching as well as his scholarship? In conferences with his advisees, does the English professor speak favorably about the profession of teaching English in the secondary schools, or does he imply that such a profession is a necessary compromise for weaker students and a tragic turn for his best students? How much importance does the English professor attach to the efforts of those who teach courses in education and in the teaching of English? If the English professor teaches graduate courses, does he welcome teachers to them or does he grumble about overcrowded graduate colleges and then say or imply that he would prefer to limit his classes to English doctoral students in residence?

As the student moves into professional courses, what is his image of the professor of education? Does this professor inspire the student with his teaching, his scholarship, and the content of his courses? Does this professor say or imply that knowledge of subject matter does not make a major contribution to effective teaching or that English is a tool subject without a content and structure of its own? Does the professor of education show respect for English professors and for English majors who may not see the importance of professional preparation?

What is the image of the English methods instructor in the eyes of the student? Is this person a former successful high school English teacher of fairly recent vintage? Does he enjoy status in his department, and does he seek and enjoy working relationships with professors of English and education? Does he seek an especially close working relationship with practicing high school English teachers? Does he inspire the student with his teaching, his scholarship, and the content of his courses?

Phase Three is the professional environment of the student teacher or intern. Does the college try to place the student in an excellent student-teaching situation and try to provide excellent college supervision by faculty members or doctoral candidates who have a strong academic preparation in English and several years of successful teaching experience in the high schools? Does the high school respect the student teacher's academic and professional preparation, and does the cooperating teacher try to provide excellent supervision? Are student teachers treated as members of the profession?

Phase Four is the professional environment of the first-year English teacher. Having reached this phase, the beginning teacher sees some new images, reconsiders old images that gave him first impressions as a high school student, and creates an image for *his* would-be English teachers. This time he will try to see himself as he is seen by the community, other teachers, his administrators, and his students. He will hope that his aims and his work are understood, respected, and appreciated; and, if he has gone into teaching with any spirit, he will begin to speak out in behalf of his students and his profession. With his students uppermost in his mind, he will seek improved teaching conditions, better teaching materials, and assistance from his school system in furthering his academic and professional education. He will earn the right to expect a salary which clearly recognizes his professional status and his individual knowledge and skills.

A very promising high school student who sees no good images, only nightmares, will never enter the profession. A college student who cannot bring many good images into clear focus will very likely be a professional drop-out or a mediocre teacher. But the emerging teacher who sees his "life cycle" as a series of clear and satisfying images to which he can personally add a few touches of color and meaning will have the best opportunity of becoming the kind of superior English teacher that the profession hopes to produce in greater numbers.

Who can say he is not an image-maker for the would-be English teacher? In its appeal to the community, the school, and the college, the profession reaches out to the entire nation for assistance in recruiting, preparing, and educating its teachers.

SELECTED REFERENCES

American Association of Colleges for Teacher Education. *Action for Improvement of Teacher Education*. Eighteenth Yearbook. Washington, D.C.: American Association of Colleges for Teacher Education, 1965.

————. *Liberal Arts Colleges and Teacher Education: A Survey of Programs, Practices, and Problems*. AACTE Study Series No. 7. Washington, D.C.: American Association of Colleges for Teacher Education, 1963.

————. *A Proposal for the Revision of the Pre-Service Professional Component of a Program in Teacher Education*. Washington, D.C.: American Association of Colleges for Teacher Education, 1964.

————. *Teacher Education Looks to the Future*. Washington, D.C.: American Association of Colleges for Teacher Education, 1965.

American Association of School Administrators and Research Division, National Education Association. *Cooperation in Student Teaching*. Educational Research Service Circular No. 4. Washington, D.C.: Educational Research Service, 1964.

Biddle, Bruce J., and William J. Ellena, eds. *Contemporary Research on Teacher Effectiveness*. New York: Holt, Rinehart and Winston, 1964.

Burton, Dwight L., ed. *English Education Today*. Champaign, Illinois: National Council of Teachers of English, 1963.

Committee on National Interest. *The National Interest and the Continuing Education of Teachers of English*. Champaign, Illinois: National Council of Teachers of English, 1964.

Committee on National Interest. *The National Interest and the Teaching of English.* Champaign, Illinois: National Council of Teachers of English, 1961.

Conant, James B. *The Education of American Teachers.* New York: McGraw-Hill Book Company, 1963.

Evans, William H., ed. *Preparing the Beginning English Teacher. The Illinois English Bulletin,* LI, No. 2 (November, 1963).

————, and Michael J. Cardone. *Specialized Courses in Methods of Teaching English.* Champaign, Illinois: National Council of Teachers of English, 1964.

Finch, Jeremiah. "College English Departments and Teacher Preparation." *Publications of the Modern Language Association,* LXXX (May, 1965), 3-7.

Grommon, Alfred, ed. *The Education of Teachers of English for American Schools and Colleges.* Volume V of the NCTE Curriculum Series. New York: Appleton-Century-Crofts, 1963.

Kegler, Stanley B., ed. *The Changing Role of English Education.* Champaign, Illinois: National Council of Teachers of English, 1965.

Knapp, Dale L. "Preparing Teachers of Disadvantaged Youth: Emerging Trends." *The Journal of Teacher Education,* XVI (June, 1965), 188-92.

"Language and Literature." *The Academic Preparation of Secondary School Teachers.* The reports of four Committees of the Twenty-nine College Cooperative Plan. Cambridge: Harvard University Press, 1962.

Meade, Richard A. *Fifth-Year and Five-Year Programs for the Preservice Education of Teachers of English: A Description of 104 Programs.* Champaign, Illinois: National Council of Teachers of English, 1964.

National Commission on Teacher Education and Professional Standards. *Changes in Teacher Education: An Appraisal.* Washington, D.C.: National Education Association, 1964.

————. *Directory of Innovations in Teacher Education.* Washington, D.C.: National Education Association, 1963.

————. *New Horizons: The Becoming Journey.* Washington, D.C.: National Education Association, 1962.

————. *The Development of the Career Teacher: Professional Responsibility for Continuing Education.* Washington, D.C.: The National Education Association, 1964.

Rosenblatt, Louise M. *Research Development Seminar in the Teaching of English*. The Cooperative Research Branch of the U. S. Office of Education, Project G-009, 1963. Available from the National Council of Teachers of English.

Russell, David H., and Others, eds. *Research Design and the Teaching of English*. Proceedings of the San Francisco Conference. Champaign, Illinois: National Council of Teachers of English, 1964.

Sarason, Seymour B., Kenneth Davidson, and Burton Blatt. *The Preparation of Teachers: An Unstudied Problem in Education*. New York: John Wiley & Sons, Inc., 1962.

Saxe, Richard W. "Evaluating the Breakthrough Programs." *The Journal of Teacher Education*, XVI (June, 1965), 202-9.

Shades, C. T. "A Study of Practices Considered Effective by Teachers of Language Arts Methods Courses in the 16 Oklahoma Colleges Accredited for Teacher Education Program." Unpublished doctoral dissertation, Oklahoma State University, 1965.

Slack, Robert C. "A Report on Project English." *The English Journal*, LIII (December, 1964), 681-86.

Slothower, William R. "English-Language Preparation Required of Prospective Teachers of High-School English in American Colleges and Universities." Unpublished doctoral dissertation, University of Illinois, 1959.

Smith, B. Othanel. *A Tentative Report on the Strategies of Teaching*. Urbana, Illinois: Bureau of Educational Research, College of Education, University of Illinois, 1964.

Smith, E. Brooks, and Patrick Johnson, eds. *School-College Relationships in Teacher Education: Report of a National Survey of Cooperative Ventures*. Washington, D.C.: American Association of Colleges for Teacher Education, 1964.

Steinberg, Erwin, ed. *Needed Research in the Teaching of English*/OE-30010 Cooperative Research Monograph No. 11. Washington, D.C.: U. S. Office of Education, 1963.

Stone, James C., and Clark N. Robinson. *The Graduate Internship Program in Teacher Education*. University of California Publications in Education, Volume XV. Berkeley: University of California Press, 1965.

Swenson, Esther J. "Teacher Preparation." *Individualizing Instruction*. The Sixty-First Yearbook, Part I. Chicago:

National Society for the Study of Education, 1962. Pp. 287-304.

Tuttle, Donald R. "Basic Considerations in Preparing, Certifying, and Assigning Teachers of English," *College English,* XXIV (May, 1963), 619-24.

Wasson, Richard, ed. *Proceedings of the Allerton Park Conference on Research in the Teaching of English.* Sponsored by the U. S. Office of Education in Cooperation with the University of Illinois. Project No. G-1006. Available from the National Council of Teachers of English.

Wiley, Autrey Nell. "Five More Years of Work on the Preparation and Certification of Teachers of English: A Bibliography of Studies for 1957-1961. Reprinted from *College English.*" Champaign, Illinois: National Council of Teachers of English, 1961.

VIII

Epilogue

Today the principal aims are to identify and describe English as a subject and to improve the quality of English instruction. New knowledge about the subject, new resources and teaching aids, new and newly revived theories of learning applied to methods of inquiry in the subject, new interdisciplinary commitments to teacher preparation and the teaching of English, and a growing general awareness, even among lay citizens, that there may be a "new English" to consider in the secondary schools all characterize a movement which is called by many in the profession a revolution.

But *revolution* has several meanings. The dictionary states that a revolution can be a complete overthrow of established procedure or order. One might ask if this is happening in the field of English. The answer seems clear. In spite of transcendental statements, which are on occasion heard in college classrooms and found in the professional literature, English hasn't suddenly executed a revolutionary coup or managed somehow to be reborn within the past five or ten years. Even the most excited new linguists and grammarians surely realize that their science and their knowledge owe something to generations of scholarship and scientific inquiry.

The dictionary also states that a revolution can be a "procedure or course as if in a circuit, as back to a starting point in time." Certainly a round or cycle of attitudes or events would set no precedent in the teaching of English. This route or course certainly does not characterize present trends, but whenever it seems evident it bears watching.

A slight diversion might be in order to illustrate this kind of cycle. For example, concern for the quality of English instruction has led the Commission on English to say of "literature of adolescence" (an unfortunate choice of words referring to literature *for* adolescents) that "in the high school years, the aim should be not to find the students' level so much as to raise it, and such books rarely elevate."[1] Although the Commission refers especially to college-bound students in its book, it has extended this statement to cover all students who are not in classes in remedial reading. In doing so, the Commission includes at least 95 per cent of the students across the nation. In view of this range of students, the Commission goes on to say that "the competent teacher can bridge the distances between good books and the immaturity of his students; that is in fact, his primary duty as a teacher of literature."[2]

An interesting parallel can be drawn between the Commission's statement in 1965 and one of the most conservative statements in the "Hosic Report" of 1917:

> Great books still have the power to strenghten and uplift, to furnish solace and good cheer. Who shall say that boys and girls of to-day will not need their clear note of inspiration and courage as much if not more than their fathers and mothers of yesterday. It is the joyous prerogative of the teacher of literature to lead his pupils to the source of permanent riches. If he fails, it is not because the wealth is no longer of value, but because he is unable to point the way."[3]

These statements stem from widely divergent convictions; the statement made in 1917 stems from the belief that literature should be studied for its "high ethical and social message," and the one made in 1965 stems from the belief that literature "must be studied on its own terms, as an imaginative construct depending for its power and persuasiveness on the deployment of language."[4] But they are in such close agreement that one might

[1]Commission on English of the College Entrance Examination Board, *Freedom and Discipline in English* (New York: College Entrance Examination Board, 1965), p. 49.

[2]*Ibid.,* p. 50.

[3]U. S. Bureau of Education, *Reorganization of English in Secondary Schools.* Bulletin No. 2. Compiled by James Fleming Hosic (Washington, D. C.: U. S. Government Printing Office, 1917), p. 65.

[4]*Freedom and Discipline in English,* p. 52.

suppose that the Commission is echoing a philosophy which was popular before much was known about adolescents.

Now to return to the dictionary for a third meaning, a "marked change in something." That English is undergoing a marked change seems quite evident. In fact, it seems likely that English is undergoing the second most significant change in its history as a subject. The first probably came about in a shift of attention after the "Hosic Report" from subject matter to student, from little attention to the student's interests, ability, and needs, to much attention to these matters. This was a shift from mastery of subject matter, with spiritual strength and scholarship as main goals, to efficient use of English as a tool subject for furthering vocational, social, and ethical aims of the nation. This shift did not come without some anxiety. During World War I, the Great Depression, and World War II, many English teachers feared that English would be swallowed by the social studies and softened by the digestive juices of life adjustment.

But English was not devoured, and the signs that this probably would not happen appeared before Sputnik. They appeared in the search for new information about the nature and use of the English language, in the search for a more effective way to teach literature to adolescents, in the search for new information about the learning process, and in the increased attention to the needs, abilities, and growth of individual students in knowledge and use of English.

Developments which have emerged since Sputnik, although not necessarily caused by that event, indicate that attention is shifting away from the needs and abilities of students and centering more squarely on the subject taught. Some in the profession would say that there has been a shift from the mechanics of education to the substance of education. It may be closer to fact to say that through the first half of the twentieth century the mechanics of education served prescriptive, deductive teaching in English; and that very recently the mechanics of education have been asked to serve descriptive, inductive teaching in English. In teaching that form and structure are one, and that inquiry into structure should be inductive, the profession may have reached its second big change, and perhaps its most significant milestone in improving the quality of instruction in the subject.

But closer attention to the subject should also raise a question. Is the subject or the student the main consideration in calling on education to aid in teaching new knowledge? Emerging developments may lead specialists in the teaching of English to wonder, as have their colleagues in "the new math," whether untested assumptions and pure theory should be carried so directly and so completely into the high school curriculum. Is the English profession, for example, in any position to say that one theory about the structure of literature, or that one new system for describing the English language should determine the content of the curriculum? Will students who have been led to examine particulars and then to formulate for themselves the latest theories on what English is and how English functions be able to communicate more effectively in a changing society and a changing world? The answer had better be "Yes."

With change grows the need to consider and reconsider each new development carefully and realistically in light of its contribution to the upward spiraling of progress in the teaching of English. But what is progress? The English teacher takes a special point of view in answering this question. From the teacher's point of view, the worth of a new development is measured in terms of its benefit to the students. Change serves students well if it furthers growth in those thought processes and communication skills which individual students, including the disadvantaged,[5] can use in realizing their potentials, and in making contributions to their changing society.

[5]Work in English with the disadvantaged has only begun, but the following publications contain some interesting descriptions of early attempts: *Language Programs for the Disadvantaged* (Champaign, Illinois: National Council of Teachers of English, 1965); Muriel Crosby, *An Adventure in Human Relations* (Chicago: Follett Publishing Company, 1965); *Promising Practices from the Projects for the Culturally Deprived* (Chicago: The Research Council of the Great Cities Program for School Improvement, 1964); Staten W. Webster, ed., *The Disadvantaged Learner*. San Francisco: Chandler Publishing Company, 1966; Forthcoming books containing results from USOE English Project at Hunter College, published by Macmillan Company.

Index

Index

PRINTED IN U.S.A.